Endors

A Church Building Every ½ Mile is a sobering and honest look at Christianity today. A must read for pastors and anyone in leadership! The manual for the new millennium!

–**Phil Fischer,** Singer/Songwriter; www.PhilFischer.com, Washington State

A move of the Spirit is happening in our day that is nothing less than a return to church life and experience as outlined in the pages of the New Testament. This book by Jon Zens is an important contribution to that end, and clearly reveals the root causes of the problems that have dogged the Christian Church for so many centuries. I commend it to you.

–**Beresford Job**, Chigwell Christian Fellowship, UK; author of *Biblical Church: a Challenge to Unscriptural Traditions and Practice.*

As I read this book, I was reminded that here in Houston we have one long block near Chinatown that has 13 storefront churches and a Buddhist temple! Thus, in less than ½ mile these have clustered to become an embarrassment to the Kingdom, violating Christ's prayer that we might all become one. Jon is "telling it like it is" for those who are concerned about the trends in church life today.

–**Dr. Ralph W. Neighbor**, Texas, author of *The Seven Last Words of the Church*

During many years I have known Jon Zens, I have found him to be a stimulating writer. Especially on the doctrine and practice of life in the church. He is willing to be radical when he finds radicalism in Scripture, to go against our accepted ways of thinking and living. Like me, he finds the denominational divisions of the church to be harmful and unjustified. So, without commending his model in detail, I can recommend this book for the direction it follows and for its stimulus to godly rethinking. I hope that it gets a lot of attention.

–**John Frame**, Professor of Systematic Theology & Philosophy, Reformed Theological Seminary, Florida

When are we going to put aside the things that divide us, accept all as our brothers and sisters, fellowship with all, return to the simplicity of the early Church, and work together to extend Christ's Kingdom? Jon Zens' new book speaks powerfully about these matters. We highly recommend it.

> –**Nate Krupp**, Author of *God's Simple Plan for His Church* & **Joanne Krupp**, Author of *Woman: God's Plan not Man's Tradition*, Oregon

I love the drift of the essays in this book. They are written clearly and incisively. *A Church Building Every ½ Mile* will be a welcome addition to a subject that most are skipping over. I hope that your book gets the circulation that it deserves.

> –**Tony Dale**, Editor *House2House*, co-author of *Simply Church*.

Jon Zens is an organic church pioneer and advocate whose depth of knowledge and experience shows in this newest work. I thoroughly enjoyed it. His section on "Four Tragic Shifts" alone is worth the price of the book! As C. H. Spurgeon used to say: 'Wear the old coat; buy the new book' ... Particularly this one!

> –**Maurice Smith**, www.parousianetwork.org, author of *You Wanna to Do What in Your House?!*

This book examines all sorts of craziness regarding this thing we call "church." Jon Zens compelled me to ponder why we do church the way we do and helped me ask brave questions of myself regarding what I will settle for. I want to welcome the stripping away of veneer and pomp until He alone remains on the throne of my heart. This book may rock your status quo but it will make you hungry for all that is pure and good.

> –**Julie Ross**, Life Coach, Simple Church Planter, South Dakota

I have been very busy in the last few years, and not able to spend as much time as I have wanted to giving my attention to reading articles, etc. Having read *A Church*

Building Every ½ Mile has strengthened my convictions and resolve of late to re-order some of my priorities, and to spend a lot more time reading, studying, and meditating on the things of God.

–**Becky Solomon**, Homeschooler, Australia

Interesting, accessible, witty, and theologically-sound, Jon's work is an important read for those who sense the deep need for the Lord's presence in the midst of His people.

–**Stephanie Bennett**, Ph.D., Professor of Communication and Mass Media, Florida

This critique of what has been calling itself "church" is the clearest, most concise and most free of wounded polemics of any I have come across to date. Jon has done us a great service, not only in the perspective shared, but in the clarity of its expression, and its freedom from the offendedness that often comes as a result of hard lessons learned. This is truly a foretaste of "... The glorious liberty of the children of God." It's all good! I mean really good!

–**Jay Ferris**, North Carolina, author of *Not Left Behind* and *The Parable of Gold*

For leaders of American churches, this book reads like a morning glance in the bathroom mirror – it shocks! But author Jon Zens has done us a huge favor. He does not leave us agonizing over our flaws, nor does he allow us to cover our blemishes with artificial success; but rather, he prescribes for us a spiritual and philosophical makeover that, if followed, will allow our churches to reveal the divine beauty that God designed us to possess.

–**Wade Burleson**, Pastor, Emmanuel Baptist Church, Enid, Oklahoma

I have heard Jon's prophetic voice often in the past 15 years. We need to heed the call to seek for the Christ-exalting alternative Jon describes. May we be exercised to respond in a way that will transform "church" and transform us as the people of God called to be salt and light as we witness by life and word to our Lord and see the increase of His kingdom in the hearts and lives of those God puts in our way.

–**Uwe Balzat**, Importer/Exporter, New Zealand

Jon Zens has hit a home run exposing the mess of clerical, denominational and issue-related congregations. Now, what are we going to do about it? What can we do about it? What does God want us to do about it? Thank you, Jon, for pulling back the covers on a big mess!

–**Frank Smith**, Crushed Grapes Ministry, California

The questions raised in this book have personally challenged me in my thinking about what we rally around as believers. The fact that traditions and thinking that were unheard of in the early church have now become accept-able norms is a sad commentary on the state of "church" as we know it today. Having personally experienced many of the issues discussed here, I have seen first-hand the damage, hurt and division that arises in the body as soon as the focus is very subtly shifted from the person of Jesus to the person standing behind the pulpit. Unfortunately, most churches have become large organizations rather than living, functioning organisms. "To those who have ears to hear, let them hear" (Matt. 11:15).

–**Hannah Hale**, Administrative Assistant, Minnesota

A Church Building Every ½ Mile is a subtle but fitting title for helping us name our shameful ways of "doing church." With compulsive regularity and lumpish complacency, we American Christians have saddled our-selves with several patently dysfunctional public practices. This challenging book by Jon Zens is a no-holds-barred analysis of the ways we have subverted the modeled behavior of the early church. He is optimistic we can do better—but only after we have taken sufficient inventory of the problems that beset us. I simply cannot imagine a better start at getting to the bottom of our corporate waywardness from New Testament strategies than by taking this kind of honest look at ourselves.

–**Rance Darity**, Bovine Reproduction Specialist, Penn-sylvania

I am pleased to enthusiastically to recommend Jon's book to every one who cares about the Church and the state of Christianity in this postmodern world. Decades of wisdom distilled from his study, his visits to other assemblies and his own labors as an elder tending over the flock make this a valuable and timely addition to the growing literature on church. Reading it will warm your heart and challenge your thinking: Jon's writing has always been a tonic for my soul during the past 15 years. Highly recommended!

–**Paul Sue**, Curator, www.BatteredSheep.com

To those like me who are re-examining the role of institutional structures in their spiritual lives, as well as those simply curious about recent upheavals in church demographics, Jon Zens offers a dose of hard, yet compassionately delivered reality in his new book *A Church Building Every 1/2 Mile*. I found myself nodding enthusiastically as I read Jon's examination of clergy in isolation, depression and burnout, recalling the countless hours my wife and I have spent ministering to pastors with no place to turn. If you sense there's something wrong with continuing "church as usual," if you're tired of self-help and "church growth" books that promise help for the church but fail to challenge its root problems, if you desire truth and are willing to have your presuppositions challenged, I recommend this book.

–**Kyle Knapp**, Singer/Songwriter, former denominational pastor,www.kyleknapp.com or www.tuesdaytogether.us Nebraska

Refreshingly absent of the bitterness that pervades similar works, this primer covers in a short space why the Church that Christ built went so wrong, how it wounded those it should have healed and why we can and should forgive those who injured us in its system. Jon encourages believers to return to life in the spirit and the "freedom to meet anywhere in which they can foster, cultivate and attain the goals set before them by Christ."

–**Kathryn Brogdon**, blogwriter at www.saltsister.com

I first met Jon in 1978, and he has been a friend and mentor for 30 years. As I read *A Church Building Every ½ Mile* my heart yearned for the simplicity to be found in our Lord Jesus. This book challenges not only the what and how of our practices, but more importantly, the why, or why not! For the world to see our revolutionary love for one another, these departures from this simplicity must be addressed. This small book is not meant as a cure all, but it furthers the discussion and increases our hunger and thirst for the ekklesia I had the joy of witnessing among the Banjaro people of India. May the Lord be pleased to visit us in the West as well.

–**Rennes Bowers**, Fire Department Captain, Ohio

The author of Hebrews exhorted us to leave every encumbrance in order to run faith's marathon. Sadly, the church has imagined itself in a parade, and has fostered many pleasing encumbrances. I too have marched as a salaried leader in the parade. Inspired by authors and examples like Jon Zens, I have traded traditional leadership for true servant-leadership. I urge believers, especially ministry leaders, to read this book with open hearts.

–**Jonathan Henry**, M.Div., Th.M., Pennsylvania

Jon Zens is not happy with the current fragmentation of Jesus' church–and on this he is squarely on the side of the angels. This is a gracious, well-researched, prophetic call for the deeper unity of the church for the sake of its witness. It is also a challenge to continue the reform of the church along New Testament lines. A great book.

–**Alan Hirsch**, author of *The Forgotten Ways* and *The Shaping of Things to Come.*

More endorsements are can be seen in the back of this book and at www.jonzens.com

If you would like to contact Jon with questions or dialog about this book, write: jzens@searchingtogether.org or call him at either 715-338-2796 or 651-465-6516.

A CHURCH BUILDING EVERY ½ MILE

A CHURCH BUILDING EVERY ½ MILE
What Makes American Christianity Tick?

And Other Essays By

Jon Zens

Lincoln, Nebraska

A CHURCH BUILDING EVERY ½ MILE

What Makes American Christianity Tick?

Jon Zens

Permission for wider usage of this material can be obtained through Ekklesia Press (address below) or go to: www.kingdomcitizenship.org

Library of Congress Control Number: 2008928597

Publisher's Cataloging-in-Publication
(Provided by Quality Books, Inc.)

Zens, Jon.
    A church building every 1/2 mile : what makes
American Christianity tick? : and other essays / by Jon

Zens.
    p. cm.
    Includes bibliographical references.
    LCCN 2008928597
    ISBN-13: 978-0-9765222-5-6
    ISBN-10: 0-9765222-5-X

    1. Christianity--United States--21st century.
    2. Christianity--United States--Controversial literature.
    3. Church. 4. United States--Religious life and
customs. I. Title. II. Title: Church building every
half mile.

BR526.Z46 2008   277.3'083
                           QBI08-600200

This volume is printed on acid free paper and meets ANSI Z39.48 standards.

Cover design by: **Mark Sequeira, MJAStudios, Gilbert, AZ 2008**

Printed in the United States of America

Ekklesia Press is a ministry to help authors get published and to publish works that are not deemed "profitable" by the mainstream publishing industry. Our goal is to put works into print that will impact and motivate followers of Christ to fulfill the Great Commission in an ever increasing way.

Ekklesia Press is an extension of www.kingdomcitizenship.org

Ekklesia Press
6709 Francis St.
Lincoln, NE, 68505 USA

Contents

*I dedicate this book to Dotty
—my wife of forty years.
She brings a special joy into life as we follow
Jesus together.*

FOREWORD

As a student of history, I've observed that the past often repeats itself. This applies to the work of God as much as anything else.

We are living in an interesting time.

The Protestant Reformation is repeating itself again. Back then, men in the likes of Luther, Melanchthon, Zwingli, and others were challenging the religious system of their day.

As a result, the Reformation changed the landscape of the Christian faith. The result: the Protestant church ended up becoming just as accepted as the Roman Catholic Church.

But that's not all.

The Radical Reformation is repeating itself again. Like the Protestant Reformers, the Radical reformers—the Anabaptists—not only challenged the *theology* of the present-day church, but they did something beyond that. They also challenged its *ecclesiology*.

Regrettably, the Radical reformers suffered untold persecution by their Christian contemporaries—both Protestant and Catholic. Yet the voices of Menno Simons, Felix Mantz, and Conrad

Grebel could not be stopped ... not until the brutal hand of martyrdom silenced them.

But that's not all.

The work of God in the 1930s is repeating itself again. During those years, God raised up a number of voices to present a deep and rich revelation of the centrality of Jesus Christ and the reality of His church. Watchman Nee in China, T. Austin-Sparks in England, and Dietrich Bonhoeffer in Germany were just some of them.

Today, we are living in another move of God. Some, like George Barna, are calling it a "Revolution."

And just like the goings of God that preceded us, the Lord is raising up a number of contemporary voices to challenge the church prophetically and bring her back to her spiritual, biblical, and Christ-centered roots.

Jon Zens is one such voice.

In *A Church Building Every 1/2 Mile*, Jon is at his best. Crisp, gracious, insightful, and compelling, this book raises critical challenges about the contemporary form of church as we know it today. It also urges us to reclaim God's original intention for His Body.

Frank Viola
Author of *Pagan Christianity* and *Reimagining Church*, Gainesville, Florida

PREFACE

In 1975 my family moved from Philadelphia to Nashville to be part of a fellowship that met in Norbert Ward's basement, and to work with *Baptist Reformation Review*, which he then edited. Little did I know that an invitation to speak at a church in Arkansas in February 1977 would turn out to be a crucial turning point in my pilgrimage. The way this body functioned was a strikingly new paradigm for me, and the elders strongly encouraged me to read Leonard Verduin's *The Reformers and Their Stepchildren*.

I read *Reformers* in June 1977 and soon thereafter Howard Snyder's *The Problem of Wineskins* fell into my hands. I've never been the same since. I began to see that the church was to be a *counterculture*—pursuing the kingdom of Christ together under the *New Covenant*.

My reflections on Christ-centered ethics were published in 1980: "As I Have Loved You: The Starting Point of Christian Obedience." The "love one another" of John 13:34 led me to see that the Christian ethic was embedded in a life of fellowship with others. My studies in this regard resulted in the 1981 article, "Building Up the Body: One Man or One Another?" This piece was warmly received by many, but led some to wish that I would be consigned to oblivion!

In 1982 we came to the conviction that the name of the magazine needed to change, so the *Baptist Reformation Review* became *Searching Together* in the middle of that year. The inaugural issue brought together seven articles, including ones by John H. Yoder and Hal Miller under the heading, "Re-Thinking Ministry in the Body of Christ."

Traveling the roads of America over the years has caused me to reflect deeply about the intense identification of Christianity with multitudes of buildings. It is my hope that the four articles in this book will help readers from all kinds of backgrounds wrestle with what "church" *is really about*, and to pursue life in Christ with others in true *ekklesia*. These four essays could each stand as individual parts, but they have been brought together to unfold vital perspectives from different angles:

- "A Church Building Every ½ Mile" contrasts the repetitive components of American Christianity with church life as revealed in the Scriptures.

- My 1999 letter to then Governor of Minnesota, Jesse Ventura, agrees with his claim that "organized religion is a sham," and points out to him that what Jesus is building is something from a different realm than the Christianity he harshly criticized.

- *Four Tragic Shifts* provides snapshots from church history to illustrate the movement from the spiritual simplicity of the early church to the institutionalized bureaucracy that came to dominate.

- *Churchless Faith* takes a quick look at some of the implications of the contemporary exodus from traditional church structures, and how the vacuum often created must be filled with vibrant life in Christ's body on earth.

Helpful suggestions for these essays have been received from many, but I want especially to thank Wilma Bell, Joyce and Cliff Bjork, Marge Porterfield and Becky Solomon for their hard work.

Jesus said, *"I will build my ekklesia [assembly, congregation]"* (Matt. 16:18). May the Lord continue to break forth with light and strength that will bring us to be in step with a *spiritual* building program that is after his heart!

Jon Zens
May, 2008

In these days of confusion,
vital clarity would emerge
from reading Paul Vieira's,
Jesus Has Left the Building,
(Karis Publishing, 2006, 276pp).

A CHURCH BUILDING EVERY ½ MILE:
What Makes American Christianity Tick?

Section 1

Why Are There So Many Church Buildings?

Have you ever noticed how many church buildings of all sizes and shapes plentifully dot the American landscape—especially in the South? Shane Claiborne recalled from his childhood, "I grew up in the Bible belt, in East Tennessee, where there's a church building on nearly every corner."[1] I remember vividly a Sunday morning years ago in Houston, Texas. During a twenty-minute drive from a brother's home to the Baptist church where I was speaking, I counted twenty-six church structures (most of which had "Baptist" in the title). I thought to myself, "Why does there have to be such a multiplication of expense and duplication of effort when in fact they are all essentially the same?"

Then in 2002 my wife and I visited close friends in Florida. As we drove around, one particular street emerged as a main artery to get to and from a large shopping center. After traversing 27th Avenue several times I noticed the number of church buildings we passed. The third time we were coming back from consumerland I asked Dotty to write down the names of the churches and I clocked the distance. The final tally was *eleven churches in three miles*. What we have in Vero Beach is no doubt a microcosm of what goes on in the entirety of American religious culture. I would like to use what can be seen on 27th Avenue as a springboard to reflect on the Christianity we practice in America. What emerges is a maze of common details that display themselves in fairly clear-cut patterns in all the church buildings scattered throughout the land.

Where Do We Start?

The Basic Patterns of American Christianity

When one looks at American churches, it is obvious that certain fundamental characteristics are always in place. Foremost of these being the "distinctive beliefs" and/or "charismatic personality" that hold a church or a group of churches together. It then follows that *a definite support system is always required to sustain that which marks the group as different.* Typically, the following elements will be found:

- Local buildings — in which to meet, practice and express convictions...

- Local leadership—to uphold and propagate the convictions...
- Local pulpit—to proclaim convictions and indoctrinate...
- Financial revenue (usually tithing)—to pay for required building and staff...
- Institutions—to train new leaders in the distinctive convictions...
- Headquarters—to administrate the organization and perpetuate it...
- Programs and publications—to ground its members and recruit new adherents...

What should be astoundingly shocking to us is that while churches are hopelessly divided over a legion of issues, *they are all united in the above components!*

Can you think of a church building that does not have a *pulpit* in it and a *pastor* behind it?

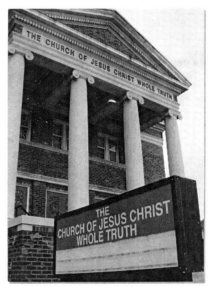

Is it any wonder why there are so many denominations? Many religious groups come across as if they have a corner on the "truth."

Section 2

Why Are There So Many Denominations?
"My Group Is Closer To the Truth Than Your Group"

That which first strikes the eye is the vast number of church buildings. Just why are there so many church structures in America? North to south on a three-mile stretch of 27th Avenue in Vero Beach, Florida, the following groups were represented with buildings: The Christian Church, Destiny Center—New Testament Faith Ministries, Faith United Fellowship, First Church of the Nazarene, First United Pentecostal, Lighthouse Church of God, Glendale Baptist, Lutheran Church of the Redeemer (Missouri Synod), Messianic Temple, Open Door Wesleyan Church and Seventh-Day Adventists.

Each building represents a group that apparently feels compelled to meet apart from other Christians because of their peculiar tradition, doctrine, distinctive or experience. Thus, if we ask, "Why are there so many meeting places?" the most fundamental answer is, *"because each group believes in some distinctive ideas which cause them to organize separately from other Christians."* If a number of churches organize around the same benchmarks we call that a *denomination.* If one church does this, it is called an *independent* church. But whether it happens collectively or singularly, it is still the same basic sin that surfaced in first century Corinthian people clustering around something or someone other than Jesus Christ himself.

One striking feature of the early church was that in each city or region it was *undifferentiated.* There were just the *believers in a city.* There were often multiple gatherings of believers in an area, but they were not *denominated.* The Body of Christ was *one.* To be sure, that *oneness* was quickly challenged by the party-spirit that emerged in Corinth, and Paul in 1 Corinthians 1-4 showed the wickedness of this error. But history since the 16th Century Protestant Reformation certainly magnifies the tragic reality of division after division. Conservative estimates would put the number of Protestant denominations at around 25,000 worldwide.

Besides the numerous times denominations have experienced this type of splintering, it is mind-boggling to contemplate the staggering number of occasions in America that *individual churches* have split apart. One church leader suggested that most Christians would experience three church break-ups in their lifetime.

The extensive fracturing of the visible Body of Christ is an enormous problem. Is it not safe to say that all the church buildings in America simply highlight the propensity to rally around agendas and not Jesus Christ alone? When will the endless manifestations of party-spirit be stopped? I believe the following observations by Robert D. Brinsmead provide a depth of insight that must be reckoned with:

> Traditional Adventism appeals to its unique doctrines as the only justification for its existence. In this it is not unlike Lutheranism, Calvinism, Campbellism [Church of Christ] or other branches of the church. Each group tends to cling to its special contribution as if that justified its existence. And generally the special contribution overwhelms the New Testament message. The only thing which justifies our right to exist either individually or corporately is the gospel . . . . The reason why Adventism cannot face the truth of history but has created so many pious legends [as have other groups] is that it depends upon that history for its corporate justification. Yet right here it unwittingly expresses its denial of justification by Christ alone. Only one history justifies our right to exist either individually or corporately—the holy history of Jesus of Nazareth. To embrace the gospel means that we confess that all history but Christ's stands under the judgment. It is His history plus nothing which justifies our existence.[2]

We cannot deny the many divisions that surround us. They stare us in the face at every turn. But are they right? How can they be justified? When will we take our stand and say, "enough is enough"? Are we able to meet in simplicity with other believers in union with Christ without reference to any distinctives that have historically separated us into various groups?

The manifestation of Christianity in America is built upon the sin described in 1 Corinthians 1:11-13 — "I am of this. . .You are of that. . . .The next person is of the other." We gather around some agenda that cuts us off from fellowship with other believers. Why are those eleven church buildings on 27th Avenue essentially islands to themselves? Because in practice each one believes that pursuing its distinctives necessitates being apart from the other Christian groups meeting on the street. Almost no group puts this thought on paper, but the truth is that each group functions as if it is significantly closer to some important truth than the others, and this perception provides sufficient justification to erect a separate building and set up shop for their brand of Christianity.

"Are all church splits sinful?" is a legitimate question in light of observing the fractured nature of Christianity in America. Of course, there are occasions where separations among believers are inevitable. But it can be safely affirmed that since the 16th Century Protestant Reformation the vast majority of fractures in the visible church have been premature and ill-founded. *Premature* in that there was little commitment and effort by the believers to work through disagreements; and *ill-founded* because separation took place on dubious grounds.

Another huge problem is that in so many church splits both sides quote Scripture to justify their contention of being on the side of truth. Those who remain cite 1 John 2:19, "These enemies of Christ were in our fellowship, but they left us." Those who leave might claim Romans 16:17, "They are against the true teaching you learned, so stay away from them." Often the truth is that both parties discredit the Lord in the way they act toward one another. More often than not, pride, self-will and malicious gossip will be found in the roots of these divisions.

The reality is that such separations are due to any combination of circumstances, but in the great majority of cases church splits take place for the wrong reasons and with very little concern to pursue *resolution* instead of *rupture*. A few separations are justified, but splintering apart should be the *exception*—the last resort—not the rule.

The pastor of this church in
Ethiopia pleaded for funds from
people in deep poverty. Why? In
order to show that the God of the
Christians can build a structure
larger than the Muslim and
heathen gods?

Section 3

Why Are So Many Resources Put Into Buildings?
The Brick and Mortar Game

Let's reflect for a moment on the financial implications of those eleven church buildings on 27th Avenue. Each congregation has to have its own place to function because of the particular emphases that separate it from other churches. This requires land and a place—and *money*. An enormous and inordinate amount of revenue is required to build, maintain and expand ecclesiastical structures. Many sources could be cited to document the extent of this problem, but for now let's consider Patrick Allitt's observations from the 1960s:

> By then [mid-1960s] the whole idea of heaping up great monuments in stone, concrete and glass was under challenge. The civil rights movement, and renewed political attention to the fact that poverty was still widespread in affluent America, prompted critics to assert that billions of dollars going to church buildings every year could be bet-

ter spent on the kind of work the Jewish Prophets and Jesus would have approved: feeding the hungry and housing the homeless. Michael Novak, a Young Turk among the Catholics, wrote in 1964 that the Catholic Church should abandon its mammoth building program altogether. . . . The time had come, he argued, "to move out of our church buildings" and "to recapture the ideals of those small groups of Christians who met together informally in living rooms, who celebrated the sacraments in small groups." The brick and mortar structure of Catholicism, achieved at immense cost over the preceding century, now seemed to him no better than a burden "which weighs us down on our pilgrimage."[3]

Keep in mind that these observations relate to the mid-1960s! Imagine the sky-high costs of church buildings forty years later in our day. I was in semi-rural Georgia several years ago, and a few miles away from where we were staying a new Southern Baptist complex had just been completed at a cost of $57 million.

Have we ever asked ourselves if Jesus—the Head of the church—would be pleased with the off-the-chart expenditure of money and resources on church structures? Are expensive buildings in line with the Kingdom of the One who had no place to lay his head? Shouldn't our financial resources be poured into *helping people in need*, rather than into *erecting and maintaining institutions that perpetuate our unique beliefs* which separate us from other believers? The multiplication of church buildings is usually *agenda-driven* and is founded on a *sectarian spirit*, not on *gospel ministry.*

There is nothing wrong with numerous bodies of believers meeting in a city. As mentioned previously, this is the way it was in the first century church. But there is a huge chasm between then and now. In the early church the various groups of Christians met separately in an *undifferentiated* manner. If you came into Ephesus, you would meet "people of the Way." Christ in Revelation 2-3 could address the "church" in each city. Now, however, we believers meet separately as *deeply fractured* and endlessly *differentiated.* If you visit any American city you will be met with buildings designating Assembly of God, Baptists, Christian Reformed, Church of Christ, Lutheran, Mennonites, Methodists, Pentecostals, Presbyterians—and the list could go on and on. Just look under "churches" in the yellow pages of any city!

The early church could meet separately in *unity*—there were no walls. Today we meet in almost total disarray and *disunity*—the walls are everywhere. In years past things were not quite as complicated. Mary Pipher reflects on the community in eastern Colorado where her grandparents— the Pages—farmed in the early 1900s. "Probably the main division in the community was between Catholics and Protestants. The few Catholic families had to travel thirty miles to church. The Pages belonged to the Congregational church that was built to include all the town's Protestants."[4]

Today most people drive past many church buildings before they reach the one of their choice. One sister experienced an extreme in this regard. "When I was growing up in Scotland among the Plymouth Brethren it was forbidden to pass an assembly hall in order to attend one that was further away. Since infighting and splits were frequent, the dissenting group would simply rent another building where they could 'legally' attend. In some cases they actually moved to another house so they wouldn't violate the rule!"

Section 4

Why Does Everything Hinge On The Pastor?

Armed with a set of separate religious beliefs and having a building in which to function, a cry similar to that of the Israelites comes into play: "We want a king like the nations!" Church people want a visible leader. The traditional role of "the pastor" or "the minister" provides the central means of upholding and proclaiming whatever it is that sets the group apart from others. What is the obvious focus of the church buildings we've been discussing? The architecture, seating and acoustics of the building all center on the *pulpit* where the special person delivers a monologue at specified times.

When individuals start chatting, they often ask each other, "What church do you attend?" This question actually implies a point of geography: "Where is the building located?" Usually the next question immediately follows on the heels of the first, *"Who is the pastor?"* People don't ask, "Do the people love one another?" or "Are they a caring fellowship?" Instead, they instinctively ask, "Who is the leader?" or "Who is the preacher?"

A Profession with a Black Hole

In the play *Smoke on the Mountain* the pastor of Mount Pleasant Baptist Church, Mervin Ogle-thorpe, announces at the start of the service, "I am the Preacher, Choir Director, Chairman of Finance, Director of Education, and Youth Director."[5] In real-life, Pastors are expected to fulfill a job description that is beyond demanding. To get their paycheck they must prepare sermons and lessons, fill the pulpit, teach Sunday School classes, counsel those with problems, make hospital visitation and pre-marital counseling, perform marriages, funerals and baptisms, bless civic events, raise money, manage staff and volunteers, resolve conflicts, be involved in evangelistic efforts, administer the Lord's Supper, attend various church (and denominational) committee meetings and functions, perform administrative duties, and generally be on call 24/7. If church attendance declines, the pastor is blamed. If it increases, it is because of his vision and leadership. The buck stops with the pastor with a vengeance. 17th Century Puritan John Owen went so far as to affirm that, ". . . on this office ['pastor'] and the discharge of it He hath laid the whole weight of *the order, rule, and edification of His church.*"[6]

This huge problem exists because the church has drifted far from its humble beginnings. Our Lord never intended anyone to wear so many hats and bear such burdens. Is it any wonder that the clergy profession is among the highest in divorce rates, nervous breakdowns, suicides, moral lapses and burn-out? A Focus on the Family survey in 2001 discovered that 1400 persons a month were "leaving the ministry."

Many in the ministry are so busy that there is little time to cultivate closeness to the Lord. The expectation is always present that they will be called upon to teach the Bible. Thus, as William Barclay pointed out, "there is the obvious danger that when a man becomes a professional preacher he is at least sometimes in the position of having to say something when he really has nothing to say."[7] Eugene H. Peterson therefore concluded, "I don't know of any other profession which it is quite as easy to fake it as in ours."[8]

It's A Lonely Road

One reason why so many clergy self-destruct is because of the incredible isolation fostered by their way of life. In the course of my seminary training it was stated in my hearing on several occasions that pastors must maintain a proper distance from the congregation. They mustn't be chummy with the laity. When you combine the clergy's insane schedule with the aloofness from those in the pew required by the profession, you often end up with a person unable to cultivate meaningful relationships—sometimes not even with his own spouse. What Barrows Dunhan noted about the exalted position of the Pharaoh in Egypt parallels what occurs in the lives of many church leaders:

> He became remote as gods are, unapproachable except by a few consecrated persons, mostly of his own family. A stifling etiquette surrounded him. He knew, in dreadful perfection, the loneliness with which power curses the powerful.[9]

Stephen G. Virginia noted that "the lack of social support and sense of isolation, for secular clergy, were key elements associated with their experience of both burnout and depression."[10]

Where Do Pastors Find Fellowship?

Since pastors can't usually find meaningful relationships among those closest to them, where do they turn? The ordained must leave their parish and attend gatherings of other ordained people. This accounts for the existence and proliferation of Ministerial Associations, Clergy Conferences, Clergy husband/wife retreats, and ministries to troubled church leaders. The clergy/laity divide creates a situation in which those on top can only find camaraderie with others in the same profession.[11]

Section 5

Why Has Church Become So One-Part Driven?

Paul said, "Now the body is not made up of one part but of many" (1 Cor. 12:14). Yet the truth is that if outsiders were to observe the way a lot of churches function, they would conclude that essentially they were centered and dependent upon one part—the "pastor." This is, in fact, the openly proclaimed viewpoint of many Evangelical leaders. David L. McKenna, for example, boldly asserted:

> [The pastor] is like the cerebellum, the center for communicating messages, coordinating functions, and conducting responses between the head and body .... The pastor is not only the authoritative communicator of the truth from the Head to the Body, but he is also the accurate communicator of the needs from the Body to the Head.[12]

In principle, isn't such a view very similar to the position of the hierarchy in Roman Catholicism? Doesn't such practice make the pastor a necessary mediator between Christ and his people?

It is this over-burdening view of leadership that is crushing many within the clergy system. No wonder the Promise Keeper's magazine, *Men of Action*, freely admitted, "Pastors are worn out, discouraged, and in need of affirmation. In fact, poll after poll reveals that most pastors are battling isolation, depression, and loneliness. They are so beaten up by the ministry..."[13] Robert McGee, author of *The Search for Significance*, noted in regard to Rapha's service to those in the ministry, "There are many wives, there are many family members of pastors and pastoral staff who don't have any place to turn, no one to talk to, no one to call up and say 'I'm hurting inside,' because we're so fearful of the confidentiality issues."[14]

The New Testament, however, envisions believers functioning together as a gifted priesthood with contributions and caring from all, thus sharing and distributing ministry so that no one person is overwhelmed. If our physical bodies suddenly asked one organ to take care of the whole body, we would be in the hospital immediately—and we would die quickly if the other parts did not resume their normal function. This being the case, how can we expect churches to be healthy when so many high-level expectations are placed upon the shoulders of one person? Christian musician Phil Fischer lamented, "Lord you give me all these gifts, yet my church still ties my hands, save me, oh won't you save me."[15]

The Pastor Is Often the Distinctive

Those eleven church buildings on 27th Avenue all have a pastor. We've already noted that the basic reason why there are eleven structures is because each group has some special beliefs or emphases that justify a separate existence. One of the pastor's responsibilities is to uphold, defend and propagate such particulars. However, in American Christianity it must be underscored that in many cases *the pastor becomes the distinctive!* When we drove by the 26 mostly Baptist churches in Houston that I mentioned earlier, the doctrinal differences between them were negligible. So why did folks drive by 12 other churches to get to the one they frequented? In many cases the answer is, *"We love the pastor and his preaching."* The truth is, then, that much of the multiplication of church buildings in America is rooted in one person's charisma, giftedness and leadership.

A great deal of the Christianity in America is *personality-based.* People will drive for miles to hear what certain preachers have to say. The life of the church is structured around the talents, vision, direction and teaching of one person. Parishioners can tolerate things like a mediocre choir if the preacher is exciting and captivating.

The Pastor's Concerns & Interests

One of the major problems of a church focusing on its leader is that the pastor's personality can become superimposed upon the assembly. As

Chip Brogden has noted, "Most pastors see the local church as an extension of their own personal ministry and calling, thus the congregation is made in the image of the pastor."[16] If the pastor grows a beard, then many men in the assembly start facial growth. If the pastor takes up golf, others get a set of clubs. When the pastor proclaims that the King James Bible is the best, the use of other versions disappears. Whatever doctrines the pastor emphasizes become the convictions of the people in the pews.

C. Peter Wagner summarizes the typical perspective on how a pastor shapes the life of a church:

> The army has only one Commander-in-Chief, Jesus Christ. The local church is like a company with one company commander, the pastor, who gets his orders from the Commander-in-Chief. The company commander has lieutenants and sergeants under him for consultation and implementation, but the final responsibility for decisions is that of the company commander, and he must answer to the Commander-in-Chief. . . . The pastor has the power in a growing church. . . . The pastor of a growing church may appear to outsiders as a dictator. But to the people of the church, his decisions are their decisions.[17]

Small, Localized Vaticans?

Historically, Protestants have criticized the Roman Catholic system for having one centralized

leader—the Pope—who can speak with virtual in-
fallibility. However, is it not the case that too many
Bible-believing churches end up with a pastor
who functions as a mini-pope? One can certainly
see from the above citations from Wagner and
McKenna that the Protestant clergy system is
conducive to fostering one-person domination.
While one Catholic Pope rules over a world-wide
network of churches and ministries, numerous
individual Protestant popes have dominion over
"independent" empires in many American cities.

Of course, there are many pastors who would
wish to be servants, having no interest in dominat-
ing a group. However, the clergy system challenges
true servanthood at every turn. It is extremely
taxing to take the stance of a servant when the
system puts the pastor on a pedestal. The buck
stops with the pastor. He has the final responsibility for decisions. The pastor has the seat of power.
The "laity have also granted clergy a special power
over God's Word by virtue of either education or
spiritual intuition."[18]

People will enter any profession with a
variety of motives. But it must be admitted that the
authority given to the clergy over the church is
especially conducive to attract personalities that
feed on elevated status, power, and privileged
position—often rooted in various insecurities. As
one who counsels clergy noted:

Sexually abusive ministers usually fit one of two profiles: the "prima donna" or the depressed pastor. The "prima donna" pastor operates out of a desire for power and control, loses touch with boundaries, over-directs people's lives, and develops a sense of "I can do no wrong".... At the other extreme is the depressed pastor, whose judgment becomes cloudy because of very low self-esteem....The high-profile pastor and the despondent minister share one fatal flaw—isolation.[19]

The clergy system contradicts Jesus' teaching in every way. It is not Christ's will for any believer to have dominion over one person (like a wife or a husband) or a group of people (like a church). Jesus taught that leaders—like the apostles, to whom he addressed these words—should live like a slave with no authority, like a child who had no status in society, like the newest person in a group who was at the bottom of the pecking order, and avoid religious titles that elevate some above others (Matt. 20:25-28, 23:8-12; Mark 10:42-45; Luke 9:46-48). In other words, they are to live like Jesus—"just as the Son of Man did not come to be served, but to serve, and to give his life as a ransom for many." The Lord was not the one reclining at the table waiting for others to bring the food; rather, he was the one bringing the fare to others waiting at the table.

Section 6

What Happens When A Pastor Leaves?

Since American Christianity revolves around the traditional pastoral office, most churches will face the repeated trauma of having to replace a pastor. The average length of a pastorate is five years.[20] Not only do pastors have reasons for "feeling called" elsewhere; they also, of course, "get the boot." In America's largest Protestant denomination, "An average of 116 of 37,000 churches in the Southern Baptist Convention dismiss their pastors *each month*."[21] How many times have the churches you've been in changed pastors?

There are variations, but usually when a pastor exits, a certain predictable chain of events is set into motion. First, a "pastoral search" committee is set up and the process is begun to find a replacement. If the church is part of a denomination, then there are prescribed procedures to follow and the headquarters will help supply candidates. If the church is non-denominational it will use advertising, the Internet, recommendations and other means to locate potential aspirants. Some congregations will seek an "interim" pastor to fill in until a full-time pastor is discovered.

When a few firm applicants initially are found, they will be asked to come with their families, one-by-one, on different weekends and preach/teach several times, spend informal time with the congregation, and be interviewed by some sub-section of the flock. When the process yields a final candidate, then that person will come again and preach, and there will be serious talk about such things as salary, benefits and housing. A congregation on the next weekend will have a formal meeting to vote on whether or not to "extend a call" to this person. If they do, then the candidate accepts or rejects "the call." If the person accepts it, then the church has to work out the details of moving this family into the community. One church announced that it might take up to two years to find a replacement for their pastor!

In many cases, losing a pastor can create a number of problems for a church. Of course, there is the ordeal of finding another pastor, which can often be a difficult, frustrating, expensive and time-consuming period for a congregation. Because so many churches are built around the pastor's charisma, it is not uncommon for attendance to plummet after this person exits. Sometimes a pastor's absence will bring about a drop in the offerings, and a church may struggle to pay the bills. There have been cases where banks will not lend large sums of money to churches unless the pastor co-signs. The banks aren't stupid. They know that the church's income is directly tied into the presence and longevity of the pastor.

Thirty years ago there was a Baptist church that experienced horrendous distress in this regard. They had grown to 80 folks and the rented building they used was too small. Through a long and drawn-out process they finally found a modest denominational church building that was for sale. After some time of negotiation they purchased the building for $65,000. On the first Sunday that they had meetings in this building, the pastor announced from the pulpit that he had renounced his Baptist convictions, had embraced Presbyterianism, and would be leaving very soon. Needless to say, a boatload of problems and concerns descended upon that assembly in a moment. The emotional wounds in the people, mostly aged 25-35, were deep and lasting. Not a few were very disillusioned. I tried—as did others—to help this situation, but it was too far gone.

A Bad System Hurts Many People
The clergy system exists in all Christian traditions—Assembly of God, Baptists, Catholic, Episcopal, Lutheran, Methodist, Pentecostal, Presbyterian,

and on and on. Even believers who theoretically reject the clergy/laity distinction often end up with a form of clergy in the way they function, even in house church settings.

As mentioned earlier, the clergy system is unrelenting in its demands upon those who occupy the offices of "pastor" and "minister." Of course, like any profession, there are those who. . . .

- Seem to thrive in it
- Manipulate it to their advantage
- Enter the field in order to gratify personal drives for power, control and recognition
- Are better than the system, but compromise their consciences in order to remain in it
- Are better than the system and end up leaving it
- Are utterly crushed and devastated by it

The traditional clergy role and all of its unrealistic demands are nowhere found in the New Testament. It puts those within its pale at risk in numerous ways. The statistics reveal that the clergy system has brought many into various kinds of ruin. Remember, around 1400 people every month are "leaving the ministry" for a number of different reasons. We can be sure that many are exiting because what they were being paid to do caused their lives and families to unravel and come apart at the seams. *The root problem is the pastor-centered system.* Anne Rowthorn pointedly observes:

Some might say it is overstating the case to claim that clergy are the oppressors and laity the oppressed. So let us make several things clear: it is primarily the *system* that oppresses. It took hundreds of years for the Church to become clericalized [taken over by clergy], and the present generation of clergy cannot be blamed for the ills of the institution they inherited. To continue to oppress the laity, however, after having become aware of the oppression *would* make them blame-worthy.[22]

J. Lee Grady recently wrote an excellent article, "Advice to a Young Leader in a Time of Shaking."[23] He gave ten points to help leaders avoid moral failure in their ministry. Some of his points were, "Live a humble and transparent life.... Stay open to correction....Don't allow people to make you a celebrity....Make family a priority.... Don't build your own kingdom." These are great suggestions, but the problem is that the people he's addressing are in a *system* that militates against every one of these important perspectives. We need to stop putting band-aids on the surface and address the system that keeps right on steamrolling over people.

When people start a church—or there is a church split and another church is formed—one of the first questions raised by the group will be, "Don't we need a pastor?" or "Who will pastor our assembly?" If the "pastor" doctrine is so vital and so central to the life of a church, why doesn't the pastor-emphasis jump out at you when the New Testament is read? Where is there any inkling in the New Testament about this one gift being the linchpin of congregational life—about one person being the cerebellum between Christ and the Body?

Section 7

Where Is The "Party-Line" Perpetuated?
Where Do Pastors Learn the Distinctives?

If a pastor is the primary herald of the beliefs and practices that set a church apart from others, then where is the leader indoctrinated in these concepts? Originally in America, ministerial trainees were mentored by seasoned pastors and often lived with them, or near them. The first seminary opened in 1784. "The ministry was the first profession in America for which a technical and standardized training was provided."[24]

The pastors of those eleven churches in Vero Beach probably were trained in almost eleven different Bible schools, seminaries and other institutions. Each school connected to a denomination or a particular ideology is committed to instill in its students the unique beliefs that brought about the institution's founding in the first place. As we look around the landscape of American religion, we need to remember that more often than not the pastor of each church has been trained at an institution which is committed to teach those within its walls the particular "party-line" it represents.

In 1985 my wife and I went to visit an old friend of mine who came from California to Aberdeen, South Dakota, to participate in his denomination's annual synod/classis meeting. Among other things, I got to sit in on an ordination meeting. The candidate sat in a chair on the platform to the left of the pulpit, while two ministers sat in chairs opposite him and worked their way through a host of questions designed to establish his "orthodoxy." What grieved my heart was that his answers sounded like an unthinking robot whose mouth moved "in sync" with a tape recording inside its metal body. He told them what they wanted to hear. If his replies had veered from "the truth" of the denomination's Confession of Faith he would have been out on his ear. He had been trained in an approved school with its party-line, and he conformed to it scrupulously in order to be accepted into the fold as a preacher.

While the average age of a person entering seminary has risen since 1990, one problem with the Bible School/Seminary approach is that this system produces graduates who generally are *young and inexperienced*. The stereotype portrays a young man who graduates from high school, finishes his B.A. at college, his M.Div., at seminary, gets married and then—after the honeymoon at around age 26—accepts a "call" to be pastor of a local church.

"Pastor/Elder/Bishop" are synonymous terms in the New Testament. "Elder" literally means "old man."[25] One has to wonder about the wisdom of younger, unseasoned people rushing into the traditional pastorate. Again, the *system* assumes that all is well with drawing from youth to fill clergy positions. It must be underscored that the *traditional clergy system is totally severed from any connection to the New Testament view of elders-bishops-pastors*. To try to apply these New Testament concepts to post-apostolic traditions is a monumental disconnect.

Secondly, in the "clergy system" Bible School/ Seminary graduates are *imported* into churches. They enter the "pastoral search" routine by coming to a church, preaching their best sermon, going through an interview, receiving a "call" from the assembly, and then accepting this "call." Such a method functionally bypasses the knowledge of a person gained through relationships in the body. It is important to realize that in the New Testament, leaders emerged from *within* a believing community. "Presbyters," Anne Rowthorn observes, "arose from the people, and they were linked with the people."[26] The early church knew nothing of *importing* an elder into their midst. Paul said, "know those who labor among you" (1 Thes. 5:12).

By bringing a person in from the outside you just can't know if they possess the character for servant leadership. The "pastoral search" practice encourages superficiality, and is often an invitation to disaster. The church is essentially inviting a person into their community whom they do not know very well.

Another problem is that this system focuses on *intellectual* attainment, not Christ-like character. Not a few have been turned away from ministry because their education was deemed insufficient. Many believe that a person possessing a diploma from the approved school (that teaches the "party-line") is equipped to lead a church. The falsehood of this assumption has been proven too many times. When I was in seminary, I cringed to think of some of these young men going out and immediately occupying pulpits. As time went on I heard of five cases where those who graduated with me had wreaked havoc in churches. Such people had sheepskins, but were not ready to shepherd.

Section 8

Why Is There So Much Focus On The Pulpit?
Where Are the Distinctives to Be Proclaimed?

In line with the focus on the pastor, it can be seen that the church service and architecture revolve around *the pulpit*. The "sacred desk" is the platform from which the distinctive beliefs of each church are disseminated. If the pastor's charisma *is* the unique feature of the church, then again the pulpit provides the primary springboard for the expression of this gift.

Is this a fair summary? *When people come to church the sermon is the climax of their visit; everything in the church bulletin leads up to the sermon; if the sermon was missing people would feel like they hadn't been to church.* Without a doubt, the sermon traditionally has been the center point.

Here is my question: *If you were to read through Matthew to Revelation twice on your knees, where would you find any evidence for, or example of, the practice of having one person give a sermon behind a pulpit?* Since this practice appears to be absent from the New Testament church, why do we get so uptight if the centrality of pulpit-preaching is questioned? Doesn't this illustrate and highlight what a tight grip tradition has upon us?

If the pastor-behind-a-pulpit isn't revealed in the New Testament, then what is? Looking at the big picture we can note that there are 58 "one another's" in the New Testament, but nothing about one person leading a church. The most comprehensive information about a gathering of believers is found in 1 Corinthians 14. There is no one leading from "up-front" in this meeting. There is nothing about a sermon being given. It is a *body* event with participation open to anyone — "each one of you has a song, a teaching, a revelation, a tongue or an interpretation...you may all prophesy one by one" (vv. 26,31). The guiding perspective in this multiple participation is, "let all things be done for the building up of the body" (v. 26b).

William Barclay noted that 1 Cor. 14:26-33 "sheds a flood of light on what an early church service was like. There was obviously great freedom and an informality about it.... There was obviously a flexibility about the order of service in the early church."[27] One question I have is, *Why have we traded the blessings of the open meeting described in* 1 Corinthians 14 *for a service that revolves around a pulpit and the pastor behind it?* We confess that the New Testament is our source for the Lord's direction in our personal lives and in our church life. Why is the revelation in 1 Corinthians 14 totally discarded in our church meetings? What is our justification for structuring meetings that are in total contradiction to what is unfolded in 1 Corinthians 14? We have elevated and canonized that for which there is no warrant, and thus suppressed and turned a deaf ear to what has been revealed. This is precisely what Jesus said would happen when human traditions intrude into our existence—"You have a fine way of setting aside the commands of God in order to observe your own traditions....Thus you nullify the Word of God by your tradition that you have handed down" (Mark 7:9, 13). Is 1 Corinthians 14 a revelation that can be set aside lightly in order to practice our pulpit-centered services?

After being a part of traditional church services for 17 years, in 1982 my wife and I experienced the joy and blessing of a truly Spirit-led, Christ-exalting gathering at an assembly we visited. Everything went wrong that morning from the physical, human standpoint. It was a cold, damp morning and people started piling up outside the rented high school building. The person with the key could not be located. Finally the building was opened, but then the room that contained the chairs, overhead projector, and everything else that had to do with setting up could not be opened. However, that obstacle was overcome and people scurried to get things in order that the meeting could start in the gymnasium. The chairs were placed in a circular arrangement around an open area in the center.

Without going into the details, the Lord Jesus was the Head of that gathering and the Spirit moved through the various parts of the Body in the singing, teaching, praying, sharing and the Lord's Supper. What cast a shadow over this particular gathering was the fact that a pregnant wife and child had been killed in an automobile accident earlier in the week. At one point the husband stood in the center and addressed the Body. What he said was incredible and affected everyone very deeply. The family we came with had to leave a bit early. After I sat down in the Volkswagen van and we pulled out into traffic, it hit me. "What an unbelievably transparent and edifying meeting that was!" I was almost numb with joy. I had never experienced anything like that. And it happened at a time least expected, when many things "went wrong," and not a few entered the meeting frustrated and "on edge."

Section 9

How Will The Budget Be Met?
"Next to your hymnals are the pledge envelopes"

With all the overhead generated by the purchase and maintenance of a building, plus staff salaries/benefits and various programs, a means of securing sufficient money from the congregation is necessary. The method used most often is *tithing*. Armed with Malachi 3:8-12—"How have we robbed you? In tithes and offerings"—many preachers proclaim the sure blessings of tithing, sometimes also emphasizing curses attached to not giving 10%.

Tithing provides a way for people to give a fixed percentage regularly. Of course, there are special projects like a building program that require giving beyond the tithe. Behind closed door meetings of church leaders, member families are often referred to as "tithing units."

The problem is that the New Testament is replete with examples of giving, but tithing is never mentioned as a benchmark. In the incidents where giving is described in the early part of Acts, tithing is absent from the narrative (Acts 2:44-45; 4:32-37; 5:1-4 and 11:27-30). The guiding principle presented was, "each according to his/her ability" (Acts 11:29). Phrases like "as the Lord has prospered you...the Lord loves a cheerful giver... according to their ability, and beyond their ability they gave of their own accord," capture Paul's outlook on Christian giving. The tithe is not present in Paul's vocabulary when he writes about giving.[28]

In many churches the pastor will say, "Will the ushers please come forward to receive our tithes and offerings." Yet nowhere in the Acts and Epistles is anyone ever commanded or encouraged to tithe. If this is so, then how can preachers spend so much time putting tithing upon the consciences of those in the pews—even threatening people who do not practice it? The emperor has no clothes! The pressure for funds to keep the religious machinery going leads them to use an old covenant model as a means to obtain a fixed percentage from the congregants.

New Covenant giving is to be done in light of Christ's giving of himself for us, without reference to percentage points (1 John 3:16-18). Believers should give generously to help meet needs, each according to his/her ability—and even beyond one's ability as the Lord leads. The Lord Jesus put it simply and pointedly—"Give and it shall be given to you, a good measure, pressed down, shaken together and running over, will be poured into your lap. For with the measure you use, it will be measured to you" (Luke 6:38).

It would appear that many church leaders have difficulty in trusting the Lord to touch the hearts of the people in light of Christ's example so they give liberally to meet real needs. This approach requires faith in God to provide. It is risky compared to the *enforcement* of tithing, which operates in terms of fixed percentage points.

Tertullian (A.D. 155-230) summarized how Christians gave in his time: "On the monthly day, if he likes, each puts in a small donation; but only if it be his pleasure, and only if he is able; for there is no compulsion; all is voluntary."[29]

Most churches are a blend of four unbiblical models:

- **Harvard**, where the professor is the preacher, the lectern is the pulpit, and the students are parishioners. Trouble is, they can sit and take notes for forty years, but they'll never graduate, never get a degree, and never ever become professors themselves.

- **Hollywood,** with its stage, entertainers, polished performances, costumed singers, applauding audiences, etc. All the church needs is popcorn.

- **IBM,** where a board of directors runs everything from the top down, where permission to do things is denied or granted by the CEO and committees, where finances are the overriding factor behind policies, and where the institution competes with other churches for market share.

- **Wal-Mart,** whose aisles and aisles of tempting merchandise offer something for everybody. Seeker-sensitive mega-churches, with their array of 100+ programs, mirror beautifully the "consumer heaven" ideal of Wal-Mart.

- **James Rutz**, *Megashift*, p. 115

Section 10

Why Is Religious Bureaucracy Created?
"Report to Headquarters"

Numerous American churches are affiliated with one or another of thousands of denominational options. The dictionary defines a "denomination" as "a religious organization uniting in a single legal and administrative body; a number of local congregations." A group of churches believe they have to be separate from others because of their unique convictions, so they set up an organizational headquarters to centralize their efforts. This staff will administer and coordinate the labor necessary to sustain existing churches, to begin new churches of their brand, to set up programs for things like foreign missions, to provide for training of future pastors, to publish books and curricula to propagate their viewpoints, and to plan activities and meetings to foster camaraderie and recruit new adherents.

Denominational headquarters vary in their methods of operation, some being very controlling and others allowing more latitude. In any event, the central office exists "to keep order" and to maintain and uphold the denominational standards. Having a headquarters, of course, significantly increases the overhead, as a building must be secured and a staff paid, among other things. In most denominations the cost for sustaining the headquarters is shouldered by required contributions from the member churches.

The Roman Catholic Church (RCC) loves to point out how fractured Protestantism has been since the 1500s, which certainly is true. But the RCC is just a huge denomination itself, a sectarian party claiming to be "of Peter." The basic problem is that each group has concluded that it possesses more of the truth, or has more revelation than others. This leads to multitudes of self-perpetuating groups and their institutions. It all boils down to what Paul spent four chapters in Corinthians rebuking—"they are of that...you are of this... and I'm of the other." Sadly, massive resources over the years have been expended to keep all these denominations going, and much of what they do creates religious bureaucracy and meaningless paperwork—not kingdom advancement.

"Independent" Churches

Many assemblies pride themselves in being "non-denominational" and "independent." However, church splits occur at a feverish pace among such churches in America. A number of these conger-

gations take on the characteristics of denominations. They become large and start sister
churches that are virtual clones of themselves, and
sometimes the pastor will speak at both. They
become the "media source" for the pastor's written
materials and spoken messages.

Such a church can end up like a vessel
floating alone in the sea with the pastor at the
helm, and it is often held together by a common
enemy or a pet doctrine. A particular view of end-
times, an emphasis on a specific Bible version, or
a commonly-held creed are examples of matters
that serve as glue to knit the group together.

Americans can be attracted to what calls
itself church by catchy signs or the promise
of needs to be met at a building.

Section 11

How Do Americans Choose A Church?

What factors are at work when a family drives thirteen miles past many church buildings and into the parking lot of the one they have chosen? When a family moves into a town, how does it narrow down the options and select a church to join? Certainly a number of concerns will enter into the choice of an assembly, but I think the following five criteria cover at least 95% of the process.

A New Believer

In many cases one who has recently come to Christ for salvation is told by a relative or friend that he/she will *surely hear the truth in their church.* This was my experience. The person who first shared the Scriptures with me invited me to his church and I was led to believe that "truth" was to be found behind the pulpit of this church.

Family Tradition

Many families have a long history of attending a specific church, or being part of a particular denomination. Family members, therefore, will often maintain the tradition by attending the local church their ancestors were part of; and if they move, they will choose the family denominational affiliation.

Doctrinal Party-Line

Those who have been indoctrinated in some particular viewpoint will seek to find a congregation where this perspective is central. Thus, they will search for a church that is "Charismatic," "Reformed," "Dispensational," "King James Version Only," "Fundamentalist," "Sabbatarian," "Non-instrumental," or "Liturgical"—whatever the specific desired characteristic may be.

The Pastor

It would appear that many folks base their choice of a church primarily on the fact that they really like the pastor's style, preaching, charisma and leadership. The presence of a popular pastor can make up for other shortcomings the church may have.

Programs

Many people choose a church because it provides services they believe are needed, such as a youth group for the teens, Sunday School for the kids, and classes for divorced people or recovering alcoholics. Anymore programs are totally diversified: there is "Christian" jazzercise, weight loss programs, and even programs that teach citizenship in the earthly realm.

The irony in all of this *modus operandi* is that when everything is boiled down, the myriad of church structures in America are generally cookie-cutter replicas of each other. The same basic elements are just poured into different buildings. The marquee by the street displays the specific brand offered inside.

One major problem with the way most Americans choose a church is that *they will probably miss the place they most need.* In order to grow spiritually we need loving contexts where we are challenged, where questions are encouraged, and where discussion is allowed. But much of the time these elements are not tolerated because *there is an agenda to defend.* People go to a building where they will hear the *party-line* and feel safe in "the truth." The doctrine espoused in each building is assumed to be correct and therefore immune to challenges. If some question it, they are usually asked to find another structure in which to meet!

American Christianity results in a situation where people are choosing one out of thousands of church buildings that are *isolated units* having very little, if any, connectedness to anything outside themselves. Therefore, individual believers usually experience no *cross-pollination* with others outside of the church in which they have placed their membership. In their best moments, every Christian tradition admits that they do not have all of the truth. Various levels of insight can be found in all theological traditions. Yet, in practice, Christian groups function as though they definitely are closest to the truth—and really have nothing to learn from other sources.

Section 12

"But Wait A Minute..."
Closing Thoughts

In the foregoing, I have attempted to set forth an overview of the key elements of American Christianity, portraying what seems to be the average experience of "church." Some readers likely are responding, "But I know of a church that is different." No doubt. There are exceptions to just about everything I have covered. However, the maxim remains true: "the exceptions prove the rule."

It must be affirmed that the Lord has worked and is working in that which calls itself "church." The Lord has converted people and built up the saints even *in spite of* a faulty system. However, we must remind ourselves that just because the Lord uses something does not mean he sanctions it. He sanctions only what is in accordance with his revealed will. The issue is not *what appears to work*, but what God has shown to be his best. I have suggested that we have sacrificed the blessed way for a substandard replacement. As Pierre Berton reminded his readers years ago, "I am not here attacking Christianity but only the institutional mantle that cloaks it."[30]

Let's think about this line of thought for a few moments in light of the history of missions. During the period of roughly 1400-1800, a form of the Christian message went out to far away places in connection with the expansion efforts of nations like England and Spain. This is called "The Age of Exploration." As explorers ventured forth by ship, the religion they brought with them was inseparably linked to the sending nation's self-serving agenda.

In the period of 1800-1970 missions arose from the efforts of churches to send people to foreign lands. While there were notable exceptions, a huge problem was created in that missionaries brought a gospel that was wedded to Western culture. Franklin Littell concluded that, "American Protestantism has persistently required that converts of the missions should adopt the food, clothing, social patterns, property ownership, and cultural values of white Western civilization." [31]

For hundreds of years God used the sacrificial efforts of many men and women to bring about much gospel fruit. However, there were also very serious and far-reaching consequences which flowed out of the long-standing practice of connecting Jesus' message with nationalistic empire-building and Western culture.

The point is this: the presence of some good fruit in a tree does not negate the fact that there may be some very serious structural problems in the root system that must be corrected.

This can all be applied to the situation with the institutional church. In spite of many unbiblical practices, and a vast waste of resources, it cannot be denied that many good things are accomplished. But it would seem that we have created a mountain of bureaucracy in place of the simplicity of Christ. We have chosen a mediocre road strewn with human traditions over the best pathway directed by signs placed along the way by the Lord.

Ekklesia (assembly, congregation) in the New Testament actually is more of an action word than a noun. It involves people with a common interest in Christ and his kingdom *gathering together* to do his will (Matt. 18:15ff.; 1 Cor. 5:1ff.; 6:1ff.; 14:1ff.). Once you define "assembly" as a dynamic context —by "who" and "what"—it is not hard to discern that a lot of what designates itself as "church" is actually not *ekklesia*. To put it simplistically, but nevertheless truthfully, *Christ is building the ekklesia, not "church."* To assume that all the buildings and the trappings we have discussed are truly "church" will not stand up to the definition and practice of *ekklesia* given in the New Testament. As Ralph Neighbor put it, "I think it is theologically correct to say that if a group of Christians who assemble don't have certain characteristics as their criteria and their foundation, they aren't a real church in the biblical sense." [32]

As I've driven the roads across America this question has lodged in my mind, *Do we really believe that the tangled mess of competing church organizations, costly buildings, church politics and bureaucracy, inordinate focus on the pastor, and endless church splits are what Jesus had in mind when he announced, "I will build my ekklesia"?* I don't think so. Frederick Buechner, I believe, has cut through the ecclesiastical fog and crystallized what I think many of us know is true in our hearts, but may be hesitant to express:

> I believe the Church has an enormous amount to learn from [support groups like AA]. I also believe that what goes on in them is far closer to what Christ meant his Church to be, and what it originally was, than much of what goes on in most churches I know. These groups have no buildings or official leadership or money. They have no rummage sales, no altar guilds, no every-member canvases. They have no preachers, no choirs, no liturgy, no real estate. They have no creeds. They have no program. They make you wonder if the best thing that could happen to many a church might not be to have its building burn down and to lose all its money. Then all that the people would have left would be God and each other.

The church often bears an uncomfortable resemblance to the dysfunctional family. There is the authoritarian presence of the minister—the professional who knows all of the answers and calls most of the shots—whom few ever challenge either because they don't dare to or because they feel it would do no good if they did. There is the outward camaraderie and inward holiness of the congregation. There are the unspoken rules and hidden agendas, the doubts and disagreements that for propriety's sake are kept more or less under cover. There are people with all sorts of enthusiasms and creativities which are not often enough made use of or even recognized because the tendency is not to rock the boat but to keep on doing things the way they have always been done.[33]

If Buechner's words ring true in your heart and you long for a Christ-exalting alternative, I would encourage you to read and put into action Frank Viola's e-Book, "Bethany: The Lord's Desire for His Church."[34] Instead of mega-churches, personality empires and agenda-based churches, we need Bethanies in every city and village lifting up Jesus Christ. For a fuller treatment of this vision read Frank Viola's *Reimagining Church: Pursuing the Dream of Organic Christianity* (David C. Cook, 2008).

27th Avenue
I must share an update about 27th Avenue in Vero Beach, FL. In 2002 there were eleven churches in three miles. Now in 2008 several have gone under, several have had name changes, and several

have been added, with the result that there are thirteen church buildings in the same three miles! And while these groups would hardly ever speak to each other, they all have the same basic churchy characteristics—distinctive beliefs, a building, a pastor, a pulpit, programs for various groups, a means to generate finances (usually tithing), a school that trains their leaders, and in some cases a denominational headquarters.

Do we really believe that what is happening on 27ᵗʰ Avenue and all across America reflects what Jesus said he would "build"? Isn't there good reason to believe "that none of the twelve apostles would feel at home in a modern church"? [35]

While John Shelby Spong himself is seriously adrift, the title of his book rings true: *Why Christianity Must Change or Die.* In 1965 Ernest Harrison stated in the Foreword to *The Comfortable Pew,* "As Mr. Berton points out, we have to consider the possibility that the Church might cease to function within the next century. He does not wish this to happen, but thinks that it will if there is no radical change."[36] And George Barna points out in *Revolution* that people are leaving institutional churches in droves to seek alternative options.[37]

Greg Albrecht recently noted that "Studies and surveys show that an increasing number of people in North America have become alienated from corporate religion—many have become disenfranchised from a denomination, feeling their church is more interested in religious tradition— or in building a new sanctuary and filling it with warm bodies—than in the authentic gospel of Jesus Christ." [38] Like it or not, many chained to the pews for years are fed up and heading out the doors to seek greener pastures.

It is evident that what calls itself "church" does not portray the picture of a healthy body—as it is clear that the church is trying to operate when most of its parts are non-functioning. The burden of ministry rests on the clergy, not on the whole priesthood of believers. How can we face why we are so dysfunctional without examining the church structures that surround us in light of God's Word? Are we open and willing to scrutinize why we continue to do what we do? Are we ready to face the possibility that "Christendom has often achieved apparent success by ignoring the precepts of its founder"? [39]

Jesse Ventura, Governor
of Minnesota from
1998-2002

A Letter To A Politician

Jesse Ventura, Former Governor of Minnesota

Preface:

When Jesse Ventura, Minnesota's outspoken former Governor, slammed "religion" in a 1999 *Playboy* Magazine interview, many religious leaders were quite incensed. I didn't know if it was worth the time to write this letter, but my wife encouraged me to send it anyway, not knowing whose hands it might fall into. My response to the Governor certainly provided a perspective that probably did not otherwise land on his desk! We don't know if Governor Ventura ever read this letter or not, but it has nevertheless gone far and wide for many other people to ponder.

Letter:

December 1999
The Honorable Jesse Ventura
State Capitol
St Paul, MN 55103

Dear Governor Ventura,

"Organized religion is a sham and a crutch for weak-minded people who need strength in numbers."

These words created quite a stir! Not a few religious leaders rebuked you, tried to defend today's religious organizations, and encouraged you to find out more about faith-based groups. I'd like to share with you my perspectives on your remarks, which probably come at things quite differently than what you've heard from other religious sources. I have wished to write you in hopes of inviting you to consider what the gospel of Jesus Christ is really about, minus the accretions and aberrations of what you called "organized religion."

So that you can better understand the context out of which I speak, a few words about myself. I'm 54 years old, work full-time at a cable manufacturer in western Wisconsin, edit a quarterly Christian periodical, and am a co-elder in a small assembly that currently meets in homes. I have a wonderful wife of 31 years, three grown children and three grandchildren. I graduated from college in 1969, from seminary in 1972, and completed a doctorate in 1983. In 1977, after reading Howard Snyder's, *The Problem of Wineskins*, I began to question many aspects of "organized religion."

Even though I'm not a constituent of Minnesota, I hope you can still find time to ruminate over what follows. I know you try to shoot straight with your words. As I also seek to mince no words, I believe you are likely to be the kind of person that is open to listen to a radical viewpoint, one that attempts to isolate several root issues.

"Organized religion is a sham." You are absolutely right on this point. What passes as the visible institution belonging to Jesus Christ is, in fact, far removed in key matters from anything the Head of the church revealed to be his will. Organized religion is a sham for the simple reason that it has — for various historical and cultural reasons — abandoned the clear teaching of Christ in the New Testament regarding the very nature of the body of Christ. The organized religion you reject, Governor Ventura, is not the genuine article. Where has it gone wrong?

Three extraordinary characteristics of the early church cover most of the territory. In each of these points what Jesus inaugurated stood in stark contrast to the surrounding pagan religions.

1. An utterly unique feature of the early church was the absence of a priestly caste. Christian assemblies had no witchdoctor, no holy man, no clergy to lead the pack. In post-apostolic history the organized church became just like other religions and elevated a clergy class above the laity. Lutheran George W. Forell summarizes this tragedy:

> Ethical guidance for people recently
> converted to Christianity . . . was offered
> at first by a polyform ministry of grace,
> reflected in the New Testament. But as
> time went by moral authority was increas-
> ingly focused on an ordered ministry of
> bishops and deacons (*History of Christian
> Ethics*, Vol. 1, Augsburg, 1979, p. 39).

The early church practiced a polyform ministry, which involved the whole body; the post-
apostolic church retrogressed to a clergy-centered
ministry.

2. Another striking element of early Christianity
   was the total absence of special buildings to
   meet in. Israel had her Temple. All of the Gen-
   tile religions had their sacred structures. But, as
   Craig S. Keener notes:

   > Believers met in homes rather than
   > church buildings for the first three
   > centuries of the church (e.g. Rom. 16:5)
   > [*The IVP Bible Background Commentary -
   > New Testament*, 1993, p. 356].

The first Christians met from house-to-house
throughout such diverse cities as Jerusalem, Rome
and Corinth. By the fourth century, however, the
institutional church became like pagan religions
and multiplied sacred buildings.

3. Until modern times the reality was that each
   nation had one religion that was enforced by

the governing powers. Religion and state were meshed. But the new community Jesus created by His death, burial and resurrection was not dependent upon state backing or defined by national boundaries. It spread all over the known world without the endorsement of or enforcement by any governmental powers. In time, of course, civil authorities persecuted the believers with vehemence.

But all of this changed with the advent of Constantine around A.D. 325. He made institutional Christianity the state religion of the Roman Empire and, among other things, used state funds to erect church buildings and to support the clergy. Thus from A.D. 325 to roughly 1700, organized religion—both Catholic and Protestant— employed the sword to maintain and propagate itself.

Once again, the visible church forsook the way of Christ and became like the heathen religions that relied on raw power to keep souls under their dominion. Eric Hoffer in *The True Believer* highlights the church's terrible compromise:

> There is hardly an example of a mass movement achieving vast proportions and a durable organization solely by persuasion. Professor Kenneth Scott Latourette, a very Christian historian, has to admit that "However incompatible the spirit of Jesus and armed force may be, and however unpleasant it may be to acknowledge the fact, as a matter of plain history [armed force]

has often made it possible for [the church] to survive" . . . . Where Christianity failed to gain or retain the backing of state power, it achieved neither a wide nor a permanent hold . . . . It also seems that, where a mass movement can either persuade or coerce, it usually chooses the latter. Persuasion is clumsy and its results uncertain (Mentor, 1964, pp. 100-101).

During the time frame of A.D. 325-1700 what did the average person think of as characteristics of the organized church? Jumping into the minds of many people would be:

1. A clergyman who runs the church
2. An ecclesiastical building
3. A religious system that holds people in its grip by the use of guilt, fear, intimidation and coercion.

Tragically, none of these elements have anything to do with what Christ's body is all about. They are contrary to the way of Christ, and rather indicate conformity to pagan religions. These three key areas where the church has conformed to worldly patterns help us to understand why organized religion became a sham.

Isn't it quite striking that the early church had its greatest period of growth without clergy, without special buildings, and without any help from the civil powers? Is it any wonder, then, that with the emergence of the clergy, cathedrals and state backing, the visible church set in motion many traditions and practices that are at odds with the Head of the church?

It is worth noting that church historians of all stripes are in consensus that the church shifted from simplicity, spontaneity and body ministry to complexity, institutional calcification and clergy dominance. James D. G. Dunn reflects this consensus when he says:

> Increasing institutionalism is the clearest mark of early Catholicism—when church becomes increasingly identified with institution, when authority becomes increasingly coterminous with office, when a basic distinction between clergy and laity becomes increasingly self-evident, when grace becomes increasingly narrowed to well-defined ritual acts. We saw above that such features were absent from first generation Christianity, though in the second generation the picture was beginning to change (*Unity & Diversity in the New Testament*, Westminster, 1977, p. 351).

If one scans what is known of the Lord's work in the rest of the world, it will be discovered that assemblies are flourishing, often with severe persecution, yet without the accoutrements of organized religion—no church properties, no clergy and no state sanction. House-church movements are strong in many places—Australia, China, Latin America, to name a few. Even in America, there is a significant awakening among many believers to the chasm between assembly life as practiced in

Paul's time and the organized religion of the day. Many are seeking to implement ways of "doing church" that reflect the "one another" emphasis in the New Testament. Home gatherings of committed believers are springing up all across our country, even in Minnesota!

I hope, Governor Ventura, that these observations help you to understand the world of difference between organized religion and the new community that Jesus purchased with His own blood. For whatever reasons, you have concluded that organized religion is a sham. But keep in mind that there is a true body of Christ that is real— albeit imperfect, to be sure. Jesus is building assemblies of believers all over the world, and the gates of hell cannot stop him from accomplishing his way.

"Organized Religion…Is A Crutch For Weak-Minded People Who Need Strength In Numbers"

The truth is that the gospel comes to people who realize that they are very sinful and cannot pull up their own bootstraps. The Holy Spirit brings them to see that they need Jesus Christ as the one who can deliver them from ungodliness. A believer is one who is brought to look by faith for a righteousness outside of himself, even the perfect righteousness of Jesus Christ.

Self-sufficient people reject the gospel. Paul, as a Jew, was such a person. He was secure in his religious heritage and prided himself as a keeper of Israel's law. But after his conversion to Christ, he looked back on all that fed his pride and viewed it as a pile of dung. He was then used by Christ to preach the gospel to Jews and Gentiles, but he repeatedly admits to his weakness:

> But I will not boast about myself, except about my weakness . . . . [The Lord] said to me, "My grace is sufficient for you, for my power is made perfect in weakness." Therefore, I will boast all the more gladly about my weaknesses, so that Christ's power may rest upon me . . . . For when I am weak, then I am strong (2 Cor. 12:5, 9-10).

This is the example of Christ: "he was crucified in weakness, but he lives by God's power" (2 Cor. 13:4). The cross appeared to be a moment of defeat in weakness, but was in fact God's way of overcoming evil and giving life to many. Jesus was killed in weakness, but resurrected in power.

Jesus' people need each other, but great numbers are irrelevant, for where two or three are gathered in Christ's name, he is in their midst. In the Book of Acts and in the Epistles the community of believers manifested a mutual care for one another. It is a sign of spiritual strength to confess that one needs the support of others in tackling life's struggles. As Barbra Streisand sang in a secular context, "People who need people are the luckiest people in the world."

The lifestyle demanded by Jesus of his disciples is difficult. The Sermon on the Mount requires the love of enemies, the turning of the cheek, and not returning evil for evil, among other things. Stanley Hauerwas notes that Jesus' commands actually highlight our need for help from the body of Christ in our pilgrimage:

> To live in the manner described in the Sermon requires learning to trust in others to help me so live. In other words, the object of the Sermon on the Mount is to create dependence; it is to force us to need one another . . . . All the so-called hard sayings of the Sermon are designed to remind us that we cannot live without depending on the support and trust of others . . . . All of these [hard sayings] are surely impossible for isolated individuals (*Unleashing the Scripture: Freeing the Bible from Captivity to America*, Abington, 1993, pp. 64,69,70).

In light of the three points which established the visible church's departure from Christ's will, you can see how organized religion, for the most part, could not be very helpful in encouraging people in a lifestyle shaped by the 58 "one another" imperatives in the New Testament. Ministry in the early church was "polyform," carried out by that which every part of Christ's body supplied. Ministry in the church by A.D. 300 was uniform, carried out by the ordained clergy who ruled over the laity.

Thank you, Governor Ventura, for bearing with me in my response to your remarks that generated such a furor from the religious community. I have tried to unfold solid reasons why organized religion long ago departed from the simplicity that is in Christ. Please understand that much more needs to be said concerning each of these points. I have just set forth the realities that cannot be denied by church historians and New Testament scholars.

Sincerely,

Jon Zens

Jon Zens, Editor,
Searching Together Magazine
(This letter originally appeared in *Searching Together*, 2000, 28:1-3, pp. 39-44)

The Four Tragic Shifts are somewhat reflected in the glorification of one task in the church and the diminution of the body ministry.

Four Tragic Shifts

In The Visible Church, 180-400 A. D.

Most professing Christians do not realize that the central concepts and practices associated with what we call "church" are not rooted in the New Testament, but in patterns established in the post-apostolic age. While there are a legion of disagreements among serious students of church history concerning various issues and details during the period of A.D. 50-325, they all speak as one voice in affirming the four undeniable shifts that will be examined in this article. Church historians of all theological and ecclesiastical backgrounds observe in their writings the following four shifts:

1. The church portrayed in the New Testament was a *dynamic organism*, a living body with many parts. The church from around A.D. 180 onwards became an increasingly hardened institution with a *fixed and complex hierarchy*.

2. The early church was marked by *polyform ministry* in which edification and the meeting of needs were accomplished through the gifts of

all the brethren. The post-apostolic church moved more and more toward a *uniform conception* of church offices which separated ministry from the "laity" and limited significant ministry to the "clergy."

3. The church of the first and most of the second centuries was characterized by cycles of intense difficulty and persecution—it was a *suffering* body. With the advent of Constantine the church became protected, favored and ultimately sanctioned as the state religion by the Roman state, and thus became an *institution at ease.*

4. Because of its dependence on the Holy Spirit the early church was very *vulnerable* from the human standpoint. There was a trust in Christ as the Head of the church to hold the brethren together and to lead them in ministry. Later, the church *trusted in itself* as a very powerful institution, along with its many rules, rites and offices to secure visible unity and obedience among its adherents.

These four shifts are indisputable. They did not come about in a day; they were the result of many factors working together as time elapsed. There are many implications to ponder in light of these significant changes that occurred. Therefore, I would like to explore each of these shifts in order to highlight certain key issues that each of us needs to face.

We claim to take Christ's revelation about the church in the New Testament seriously, yet the reality is that too often we are more attached to *the inherited way of doing things*—which is based on human traditions. What does it mean to be faithful to the New Testament's teaching about the church? In what sense are the examples of the church life "binding" on us?

For instance, some assert that since the early church met primarily in homes, we are obliged to emulate this example. I think the *primary* theological point of the New Testament in this regard is that under the New Covenant there are no alleged "holy places." Contemporary Christianity has almost no grasp of this significant point. Taking their cue from the Old Covenant, people are still led to believe that a church building is "the house of God." In actuality, believers are free to meet anywhere in which they can foster, cultivate and attain the goals set before them by Christ.

The problem today is that many church structures neither promote nor accomplish Christ's desires for His body. Homes are a natural place for believers to meet, and the early church flourished well into the first and second centuries without erecting any temple-like edifices. In places around the world where persecution reigns, house-church movements have flourished. Someday in America, if our religious infrastructure falls as a result of economic and political turmoil, true believers will be forced to meet outside of traditional church buildings. But the issue still is not what type of place believers gather in, but *what form their committed life together* takes as they wrestle with the many duties and privileges flowing out of the priesthood of all believers.

I believe that it is far more important to capture the *spirit* of church life as we see it unfolded in the New Testament than it is to attempt to woodenly replicate certain cultural aspects of first century life. We do not live in the first century, but the *concepts and principles* in the New Testament endure and will come to expression in any culture. The four tragic shifts about to be examined will give all of us plenty to reflect and act upon as we seek to take our discipleship seriously. Christians must take their stand and devote their precious energies to building up the body of Christ in ways that return to the original patterns of the New Testament.

The Shift from the Body of Christ as a Dynamic Organism to the "Church" as a Settled Institution

In 1 Corinthians 12, Paul goes into some detail concerning the implications of the church being a living organism, a body with many parts. In the early chapters of Acts we see a vibrant, caring, sharing and witnessing body of believers created by the power of the Spirit who was poured out by the risen Christ. This corporate "new man" created by Jesus was not without leadership and organization in the first century. However, there is no evidence of desire by the leaders to create a tightly-knit religious institution with an elaborate hierarchy and intricate "chain-of-command." The leaders, above all, were to be *servants* to feed and build up the flock. Any organization that emerged was for the purpose of meeting people's needs, not to create a religious bureaucracy.

The church Christ purposed to build is always described in terms of "koinonia," a common sharing of life together in the bonds of Jesus Christ. However, the reality is that as time went on after the apostles' death, the church gravitated increasingly toward finding its essential definition not in a *dynamic organism,* but in a *visible institution with a hierarchy of officers.* The church came to be no longer identified as a body of believers bonded by love, but as a religious organization whose *officers* gave it significance. Ultimately, it was asserted that *without the officers there was no church.* Organization usurped vital life as the hallmark of the church.

This legacy still remains with us today. The needs of people are subordinated to the maintenance of religious bureaucracy. Patterns of church government often have nothing to do with the ethos of the New Testament. Many define the "true" church in terms of outward marks such as "the proper preaching of the Word, the administration of the sacraments, and the practice of discipline." But these characteristics can be outwardly present in churches, and yet they can in truth be dead as a rock. The New Testament defines the church *dynamically* in terms of functioning together as a body. If church were defined, for example, in the organic terminology of Acts 2:42-47—"devoted to apostolic teaching, prayer and fellowship in the breaking of bread"—how many churches would we be left with? Why is it that even today when somebody asks "What church do you attend?," the next question normally is, "Who is the pastor there?" We still tend to define church in terms of *leadership*, rather than by *loving relationships among the brethren*.

The Shift from Polyform Ministry to Uniform Ministry

In the early church, ministry was conceived of in terms of Ephesians 4:16, "From Him the whole body, joined and held together by every supporting ligament, grows and builds itself up in love, as each part does its work." Ministry was seen as given to the *whole body* by Christ. As Paul put it, "Now the body is not made up of one part but of many....As it is, there are many parts, but one body" (1 Cor. 12:14, 20). To every person in the body of Christ is given a manifestation of the Spirit for the benefit of all (1 Cor. 12:7). The resurrection of Christ ensured that every person in the body would be gifted, which included important *equipping gifts* such as pastors-teachers (Eph. 4:7-8, 11).

The great tragedy is that from about A.D. 180 onwards the increasingly institutionalized church began to assign ministry more and more to the officers (the *clergy*) and less and less to the common people (the *laity*). George W. Forell astutely summarizes the shift from body-ministry to bishop-ministry:

> Ethical guidance for people recently con-verted to Christianity and likely to bring a perva-sive pagan attitude to his new life was offered at first by a polyform ministry of grace, reflected in the New Testament. But, as time went by, moral authority was increasingly focused on an ordered ministry of bishops and deacons.... The institu-tion most effective in containing the threats to the unity of the nascent Christian movement was the gradually evolving office of the bishop.... Through the office of the bishop the shape of the Christian life is determined and the masses recently brought into the Christian movement are conformed to Christ.[1]

The New Testament places *no emphasis* on one person who occupies the office of bishop (pastor). While it certainly contemplates a plurality of leaders as part of life in Christ's body, the overwhelming emphasis falls upon exhortations that involve all the members of the body. At least 58 times in the New Testament believers are commanded to fulfill responsibilities relating to "one another." Since then, we have turned the tables and viewed ministry as essentially resting upon "the minister" and forgotten that ministry as unfolded in the New Testament is spread around to everyone.

If ministry is not seen as focused in one office in the New Testament, where was precedent for a *separate caste* found? It was found in the exclusive priesthood under the Old Covenant. William Bausch confirms this point:

> Our survey has shown us that no cultic priesthood is to be found in the New Testament. Yet we wound up importing Old Testament Levitical forms and imposing them on Christian ministry.[2]

The negative results that arose from the shift from polyform to uniform ministry are myriad. The mutual care so basic to the fabric of early church life was virtually lost. Why? Because mutuality—"you are all brethren"—was buried beneath the superstructure of institutionalized officers. William Bausch crystallizes this point by saying,

> Nevertheless in practice there is no denying that there has historically been a gathering into one person and his office what were formerly the gifts of many. . . . [This practice] goes astray, of course, when it translates to mean that only ordination gives competence, authority, and the right of professional governance. It goes further astray when eventually all jurisdictional and administrative powers in the church come to be seen as an extension of the sacramental powers conferred at ordination. In short, there is a movement here away from the more pristine collaborative and mutual ministries of the New Testament.[3]

We must face the fact that the traditions regarding church government and order which we have inherited are cast in very suspicious garb. They are clergy-centered and generally stifle and suppress the "one another" perspectives of the New Testament. Servant leadership should be a natural part of body-life by which the people of God are encouraged and equipped for all kinds of ministry. Unfortunately, however, the shift from polyform to uniform ministry has created the deplorable situation in which the church forever remains as a dependent, helpless, non-maturing infant for the sake of the officers who watch over the crib. We have inherited traditions in which the tail wags the dog. It is my conviction that because of the deep-seated nature of this tragic shift in perspective, the greatest practical need facing the church today is the return to "a polyform ministry of grace."

The Shift from a Suffering Church to Institution of Ease

The early church grew and prospered incredibly without having church buildings or being protected by the state. In fact, from apostolic times to the rise of Constantine to power the church went through cycles of intense persecution spearheaded by the ruling powers. These times of persecution are well documented in such books as *Persecution in the Early Church* by H. B. Workman,[4] and *Martyrdom and Persecution in the Early Church* by W. H. C. Frend.[5]

However, the advent of Emperor Constantine in A.D. 312 brought great changes, most of them for the worse. Money from state funds was used to support both Christian church buildings and Christian clergy. Ultimately, Christianity was declared to be the state religion. From Constantine onwards, the visible church became enmeshed in political intrigue, and the state had its hand in the determination of church affairs. As Louis Berkhof notes regarding the Council of Nicaea in A.D. 325 (which Constantine convened and presided over):

> A settlement forced upon the Church by the strong hand of the emperor could not satisfy and was also of uncertain duration. It made the determination of the Christian faith dependent on imperial caprice and even on court intrigues. . . . The sequel clearly proved that, as it was, a change in emperor, and altered mood, or even a bribe, might alter the whole aspect of the controversy. This is exactly what happened repeatedly in subsequent history.[6]

Constantine set in motion the ideal of a territorial state religion with Christianity at the helm. This ideal was the death knell of all that the Gospel stood for. It signaled the end of believers gathering separately from the pagan culture as a counter-culture where the way of Christ was displayed in simplicity. Now the church was conceived of as all the people of a nation—at birth made both citizens of the state and constituted as part of the visible church by infant baptism. Church and politics were mixed together, creating immense confusion. Ron VanOverloop notes this phenomenon in operation from the post-apostolic church to the Reformation:

> As was the case in the early church when emperors called the great ecumenical councils together, so was the progress of the Reformation to a great extent determined by the political maneuvering taking place in each country.[7]

Whereas in the early church the disciples banded together in homes and other places as communities "called out" from the world, under Constantine this distinction was erased and "church" became defined as all citizens in a given territory. This had the practical effect of watering down true discipleship, and creating a powerless, nominal Christianity. Werner Elert contrasts the early days with the rise of Constantinianism:

> [In the early church] the strength of their ties with one another is matched by the strength of the boundary they draw to the outside. In business dealings with one another they do not choose an unbeliever to arbitrate; they transact their business "before the saints" and between "brother and brother" (1 Cor. 6:1-5). One is to throw in one's lot with those who fear the Lord, consider their common good, and daily visit the saints face to face . . . . After Constantine things changed radically with the influx of the masses. This did not prosper the Christian brotherhood. If we can believe only half of what Salvian says,

there was not much left of it a hundred years later in many parts of western Christendom.[8]

The shift from a suffering church to an institution sanctioned and promoted by the state highlights this crucial question: "Was the Constantinian change the rise or fall of the church?" How this question is answered will greatly determine one's whole view of the church and its mission. In light of New Testament revelation about the church Christ purposed to build, I submit that Constantinianism was a wretched stone thrown into the sea of church history, the ripples of which still lap upon our shores today.

We must make a choice: Are we going to cast our lot with the New Testament vision for the body of Christ (simplicity, suffering, servanthood), or with the Constantinian model (powerful institution, clergy dominance, rule by political maneuvering)? Are we going to devote the energies of our short life-span to perpetuating the post-apostolic shifts that moved away from the simplicity of Christ, or to restoring the spirit of the New Testament vision?

The Shift from a Spirit-Dependent Church to a Letter-Driven Institution

Twice in his epistles Paul refers to the fact that the church serves Christ "in [the] newness of the Spirit and not in [the] oldness of the letter" (Rom. 7:6 and 2 Cor. 3:6). The church was a community of the Spirit from the Day of Pentecost. In light of this reality, the early church did not trust in fixed forms to maintain and guard her existence. There was an openness in the body to be *Spirit-led* by light of Christ's *Gospel-word*.

This can be seen, for example, in the glimpse of an early church gathering revealed in 1 Corinthians 14. William Barclay isolates these important points from 1 Corinthians 14:

> [Paul] is determined that anyone who possesses a gift should receive every chance to exercise that gift, but he is equally determined that the services of the Church should not thereby become a kind of competitive disorder.... There must be liberty but there must be no disorder.... There was obviously a freedom and an informality about [this service] which is completely strange to our ideas.... Clearly the church had no professional ministry.... It was open to anyone who had a gift to use that gift.... There was obviously a flexibility about the order of service in the early church which is now totally lacking. There was clearly no settled order at all. Everything was informal enough to allow any man who felt that he had a message...to give it.... The really notable thing about an early Church service must have been that almost everyone came feeling that he had both the privilege and the obligation of contributing something to it.[9]

Edification was the goal which was to be reached by the Spirit-led participation of the body. The two-sided balance Paul desired can perhaps be summed up like this: no structure in the service must be allowed to stifle the free expression of edifying gifts in the body; no expression of spontaneity in the body must be allowed to blossom into unprofitable disorder.

Unfortunately, as time went on this Spirit-dependence gave way to more and more fixed forms of worship, which phased out body participation and limited "ministry" only to an ever-growing web of ecclesiastical hierarchy. By A.D. 250 church order was set in concrete, with one bishop ruling over various territories. The momentum of this church bureaucracy was accelerated when Constantine and his successors sanctioned the church and contributed money and resources to this increasingly powerful institution. What began as a Spirit-led organism ended up as a letter-dependent institution. The leaders no longer trusted in the Spirit to hold the body together; instead they leaned on intricate human contrivances and rules to give the outward appearance of unity.

One of the saddest features of this shift to letter-dependence, combined with the church's new collusion with the state, was the use of coercion—both to gain and maintain adherents. Simply trusting in the Spirit would have resulted in a spiritual reality too vulnerable to be controlled by human schemes. The use of raw power, backed by the weapons of the state, appeared to promise greater stability. Eric Hoffer makes this tragic observation, which church history unfortunately verifies:

> There is hardly an example of a mass movement achieving vast proportions and a durable organization solely by persuasion. . . . It was the temporal sword that made Christianity a world religion. Conquest and conversion went hand in hand. . . . Where Christianity failed to gain or retain the backing of state power, it achieved neither a wide nor permanent hold. . . . It also seems that, where a mass movement can either persuade or coerce, it usually chooses the latter. Persuasion is clumsy and its results uncertain.[10]

Again we must ask ourselves: Are we going to continue perpetuating the paradigm of trusting in outward carnal mechanisms to hold the church together, or will we return to a *child-like trust* in the *Spirit of Christ* to build and sustain His body?

Concluding Remarks

We have examined four clear shifts in early church history. These shifts are acknowledged by church historians of all theological persuasions. James D. G. Dunn, one of the foremost New Testament scholars of our time, summarizes the essence of these four shifts like this:

> Increasing institutionalism is the clearest mark of early Catholicism—when church be-

comes increasingly identified with institution, when authority becomes increasingly coterminous with office, when a basic distinction between clergy and laity becomes increasingly self-evident, when grace becomes increasingly narrowed to well-defined ritual acts. We saw above that such features were absent from first generation Christianity, though in the second generation the picture was beginning to change.[11]

"Such features were absent from first generation Christianity" means that *they cannot be found in the New Testament.* Does this crucial revelation concern you? Is your heart burdened having seen the chasm between the original work of the Spirit and the hardened institution that quickly emerged in the post-apostolic days? Does it bother you that most of what we associate with "church" has little to do with the New Testament, and more to do with patterns that reflect a drift away from it?

Further—and this is the key question—*Were the shifts we have studied a faithful extension of New Testament ideals, or a tacit denial of all that they stand for?* If the answer is "denial," then it is incumbent upon believers to work for the recovery of Christ's ways and to stop contributing to the perpetuation of non-edifying ecclesiastical patterns.

I commend my thoughts on these four shifts to your discerning conscience. May the Lord guide you into appropriate responses as "the worthy walk" is set before us in the Gospel.

"A Churchless Faith"

Coments on a Review

There was a good review article in *Crux* magazine (41:3, Fall, 2005), which comes out of Regent Seminary in Vancouver, BC, Canada. The book reviewed was *A Churchless Faith: Faith Journeys Beyond the Churches* by Alan Jamieson. It was reviewed by an M.Div. student, Jonathan Ryan (he goes by moniker Jono), from Wellington, NZ called, "A Churchless Faith? Alan Jamieson & Palliative Care for the Church in New Zealand," pp.29-35. Jono makes many sound points, but I think in asserting that "the church" is important in the Christian life, he makes the fatal error of assuming that what exists as "church" is what believers must "be a part of" in order to avoid spiritual catastrophe.

Jono starts off by observing, "The church's 'centre of gravity' has shifted. While the church in the Two-Thirds World currently enjoys unprecedented renewal in a diverse range of ecclesial settings, the church in the West instead battles an existential crisis, reckoning with steadily diminishing membership." He then points out that in response to this crisis, some call for reform and others call for exiting the institutions. He notes that one common opinion is that "in the same sense that Western society has become postmodern—our society has become post-church."

Alan Jamieson has written on the rapid church decline in New Zealand, *Churchless Faith* (2002). He focuses on "church leavers." Jono suggests that Jamieson's "prognosis is at best a palliative one, trying to keep it alive by maintaining its satiating diet of individualism, consumerism and care." Jamieson interviewed 108 church leavers, and noted five characteristics of these people: Disenchantment, Disillusionment, Disengagement, Disidentification and Disorientation.

After they leave, Jamieson identifies four post-church experiences: "Disillusioned Followers," "Reflective Exiles," "Transitional Explorers," and "Integrated Wayfinders." Jono responds by noting, "Alluding to the popular 'seeker-sensitive churches' of the nineties, [Jamieson] suggests the need for 'leaver-sensitive church'—'one that is aware of and seeks to address the concerns of leavers and potential leavers. . . . The leaver-sensitive church provides: places for people to explore, question and doubt; a theology of the journey; resources for people experiencing dark places; models of other theological understandings . . . ."

Most of the "leavers" Jamieson spoke with wanted to be in groups with other post-church people—groups that "are not connected to any institutional form of the church or church structures." Jamieson sees the "individual wayfarers" as roosting in "waystations," and it is in such groups that he finds hope for the church's future. Such "waystations," he observes, "are very strong communities of care, friendship, accountability, humor and depth . . . . But an equally common theme was 'safety.' Variations on the theme—'the group provides a safe place where I can be myself'—turn up."

Jono is afraid that those exiting the ranks of the institutional church are in some way jeopardizing their souls, but the flip-side must be firmly stated also, namely, that many are finding their spiritual life in danger by remaining in the status quo church. Jono wrongly assumes that the numerous buildings calling themselves "churches" are the context in which spiritual growth will take place. That simply is not the case. *Ekklesia* is a dynamic concept that is defined by certain action words (for example, 58 "one-anothers"), and cannot be confined to institutional sanctuaries.

It would be my observation that those leaving institutional churches confess their need for the body of Christ and are seeking to find *ekklesia* "reality" with others in informal settings. The truth is, you cannot put these spiritual dynamics into a box. The following observations are also true, depending on folks' circumstances:

1. People in institutional churches can sometimes find enough reality to keep them going
2. People can dry up in churchy institutions, and find reality in committed groups outside the gates of formal religion
3. People can leave traditional churches and dry up by not finding reality anywhere
4. People can leave formal church, become part of an informal group, and run into the same problems, or worse, than they encountered in the institutional setting

Whatever the options may be, the truth is that myriads of believers are tired of traditional church. They are asking some serious questions about what church is, and they are often seeking alternative answers outside of religious buildings and institutions.

In addition to Jamieson, my own research and that of other diverse sources such as Focus on the Family and George Barna have documented that people are leaving traditional churches by the droves in America and in Europe. And this trend is not particularly new. Several years ago Focus on the Family did a comprehensive study and found that 1400 persons a month were "leaving the ministry." Disregarding all the sociological observations that can be made, the fact remains that Jesus is building a living *ekklesia* which can come to expression in any number of physical settings. In such contexts these base-line attributes will be present to some degree—

1. A caring, welcoming, informal atmosphere where people are accepted in the bonds of Christ and his gospel
2. A context where Christ is the focus
3. Where relationships are being deepened
4. Where the truth can be spoken in love
5. Where healing can be experienced
6. Where gifts can be encouraged
7. Where various ministries are developed
8. Where people can share their questions and concerns
9. Where problems and disputes can be worked out
10. Where there is a growing commitment to one another to carry out a wide range of kingdom responsibilities

Genuine *ekklesia* is essentially a group of believers "fleshing out" a life of love together underneath the banner of Christ, the Head of the church.

If the places called "church" block the reality of *ekklesia* with their traditions and structures, people are going to leave. Although finding greener pastures is not always easy, it will be done by hungry people. *Ekklesia* is not automatically realized by leaving a "churchy" building and meeting in a living room. It will be a reality wherever people are seeking Christ and his will together in increasingly committed relationships.

Most of the New Testament makes no sense without the context of Christ-centered relationships. For example, Jesus said that if a disciple was hardened in sin after being encountered privately and with several present, "tell it to the *ekklesia*" was the final step (Matt. 18:15-20). This kind of kingdom labor can only blossom in the setting of the kind of caring community briefly sketched above. Christians should ask themselves, "If I fell into sin, what *ekklesia* exists in my life where my problem could be lovingly handled?"

Framing the issue this way forces each of us to realize that *true ekklesia is hard to find in our culture* and *we desperately need to establish koinonia (fellowship) in our lives*. Thomas Dubay beautifully captures the vital dimensions of our participation in the New Creation, the *ekklesia*:

[T]he biblical concept of community seems too good to be true....Loving is caring. Deep love is deep caring....The best way I can summarize what I sense to be the New Testament concept is to use an inelegant expression: to care is to jump into the other's skin. It is to become the other in mind and heart, to live the other's interests. To care is to become one's brother, one's sister....Persons in community are vibrantly present to one another. A mere formality will never do....We are interested [in others] when we are eager to listen (how many of us are *eager* to listen?) and slow to speak (James 1:19)....A caring community is a listening community....We are weak. All of us. We are to find in this mutual enheartenment an antidote to our waywardness, to our being hardened by the lure of sin (Heb. 3:13). The Christian must find the power to be what he is in the very midst of community.... Which is to say that we cannot care, we cannot have community without the Lord living in the midst of the two or three gathered in his name.... Caring is an inner sincerity of concern that enfleshes itself in all sorts of ways—expressing affection, using suitable terms of endearment, sincere concern, reverent courtesy, active mercy, never hurting, frequently encouraging, praising; it is showing a warm hospitality, a cheerful gentleness, a comforting compassion, a sincere greeting. ...There is a new relationship, a new vine flow, that of grace....Hell is non-community (*Caring: A Biblical Theology of Community*, Dimension Books, 1973, pp.8, 55, 57, 67, 72, 77, 80-81, 83, 90)

ST. CLOUD
Church of Christ
ESTABLISHED IN JERUSALEM 33 A.D.

There is no better example of
sectarian arrogance!

Further Reading and Study

Allen, Donald R. (1973). *Barefoot in the Church: Sensing the Authentic Through the House Church*, John Knox Press, 188pp.

Armstrong, Ben (1979) *The Electric Church*, Thomas Nelson, 191pp.

Arterburn, Stephen & Felton, Jack (2000) *More Jesus Less Religion: Moving from Rules to Relationship*, WaterBrook Press, 207pp.

Ault, James M., Jr. (2004) *Spirit & Flesh: Life in a Fundamentalist Baptist Church*, Knopf, 435pp.

Barna, George (2005) *Revolution: Finding Vibrant Faith Beyond the Walls of the Sanctuary*, Tyndale, 144pp.

Barna, George (1998) *The Second Coming of the Church: A Blueprint for Survival*, Word, 223pp.

Bausch, William J. (1997) *The Parish of the Next Millennium*, Twenty-Third Publications, 304pp.

Beach, Waldo (1969) *Christian Community & American Society*, Westminster Press, 190pp.

Berton, Pierre (1965) *The Comfortable Pew: A Critical Look at Christianity & the Religious Establishment*, Lippincott, 137pp.

Bouma, Mary LaGrand (1980) "Ministers' Wives: The Walking Wounded," *Leadership*, 1:1, pp.63-75.

Brunner, Emil (1952) *The Misunderstanding of the Church*, Lutterworth, 132pp.

Burke, Spencer, ed., (2007) *Out of the Ooze: Unlikely Love Letters to the Church from Beyond the Pew*, NavPress, 220pp.

Chrnalogar, Mary Alice (2000) *Twisted Scriptures: Breaking Free from Churches that Abuse*, Zondervan, 297pp.

Coalter, Milton J., et al., eds., (1990) *The Mainstream Protestant "Decline": The Presbyterian Pattern*, Westminster/ John Knox, 263pp.

Crosby, Michael H. (1991) *The Dysfunctional Church: Addiction & Codependence in the Family of Catholicism*, Ave Maria Press, 256pp.

Dawn, Marva J., (1997) *Truly the Community: Romans 12 & How to Be the Church*, Eerdmans, 303pp.

Dailey, Franklin J., (1999) *How the Catholic Church Is the*

Same & How It Is Different from Other Christian Churches, The Book Butler, n.d., 95pp.

Earle, Nick (1961) *What's Wrong with the Church?* Penguin Books, 156pp.

Ellul, Jacques, (1986) *The Subversion of Christianity*, Eerdmans, 212pp.

Engelbrecht, Douglas J. (2000) "It's Not Easy Being Short: Called Worker Shortage," *Forward/NL*, June, pp.8-9. "Although vacancy pastors from nearby congregations can help, it is just not the same as when a congregation does not have its own pastor . . . . When a congregation is vacant [without a pastor], it reminds the communicants of the royal priesthood of all believers, and spurs them on to carry out as much of the work of the ministry in that congregation as they are able to do."

Enroth, Ronald (1994) *Recovering from Churches that Abuse*, Zondervan, 166pp.

Eskridge, Larry & Noll, Mark A., eds., (2000) *More Money, More Ministry: Money & Evangelicals in Recent North American History*, Eerdmans, 429pp.

Fitch, David (2007) "Sayonara, Senior Pastor," Feb.19, , blog.christianitytoday.com/outofur/archives/2007/02/sayonara_senior.html.

Flake, Carol (1984) *Redemptorama: Culture, Politics & the New Evangelicalism*, Anchor Press, 300pp.

Frame, John (1991) *Evangelical Reunion: Denominations & the Body of Christ*, Baker, 185pp.

Garrison, Becky (2006) *Red & Blue God, Black & Blue Church: Eyewitness Accounts of How American Churches Are Hijacking Jesus, Bagging the Beatitudes, and Worshiping the Almighty Dollar*, Jossey-Bass, 176pp.

Gehring, Roger W. (2004) *House Church & Mission: The Importance of Household Structures in Early Christianity*, Hendrickson Pub., 408pp.

Gregory, Joel (1994) *Too Great A Temptation: The Seductive Power of America's Super Church*, The Summit Group, 332pp.

Haag, Herbert (1998) *Upstairs, Downstairs: Did Jesus Want A Two-Class Church?* Crossroad Publishing, 110pp.

Hadden, Jeffrey K. & Shupe, (1988) Anson *Televangelism:*

Power & Politics On God's Frontier, Henry Holt, 325pp.

Hammand, Mary Tuomi (2001) *The Church & the Dechurched: Mending A Damaged Faith*, Chalice Press, 189pp.

Hart, D.G. (2002) *That Old-Time Religion in Modern America: Evangelical Protestantism in the 20th Century*, Ivan Dee, 246pp.

Hawley, Monroe E. (1976) *Redigging the Wells: Seeking Undenominational Christianity*, Quality Publications, 224pp.

Hendricks, William D. (1993) *Exit Interviews: Revealing Stories of Why People Are Leaving the Church*, Moody, 305pp.

Hiltner, Seward (1969) *Ferment in the Ministry: A Constructive Approach to What the Minister Does*, Abingdon, 222pp.

Holl, Adolf (1974) *Jesus in Bad Company*, Discus Books, 191pp.

James, Rick (2007) *Jesus Without Religion: What Did He Say? What Did He Do? What's the Point?*, IVP, 141pp.

Johnson, David & VanVonderen, Jeff (1991) *The Subtle Power of Spiritual Abuse*, Bethany House, 234pp.

Johnson, James L. (1980) "The Ministry Can Be Hazardous to Your Health," *Leadership*, 1:1, pp.33-38.

Kallen, Horace M. (2000) "Buildings, Clergy & Money," *Searching Together*, 28:1-3, pp.25-38 [Excerpts from *Why Religion?* 1947].

Kavanaugh, James (1967) *A Modern Priest Looks At His Outdated Church*, Trident Press, 200pp.

Kennedy, Eugene (2002) *The Unhealed Wound: The Church & Sexuality*, St. Martin's Griffin, 214pp.

Kraeuter, Tom (1998) *If Standing Together Is So Great, Why Do We Keep Falling Apart? Real Answers to Walking in Unity*, Training Resources, 161pp.

Kung, Hans (1972) *Infallible? An Inquiry*, Image Books, 235pp.

Lehmann, Johannes (1974) *The Jesus Establishment: How the Church Lost Its Ideal*, Doubleday, 212pp.

Martin, Janet L. & Nelson, Suzann (1997) *Growing Up Lutheran: What Does This Mean?*, Caragana Press, 227pp.

McIntosh, Gary L. & Edmondson, R.L. (1998) *It Only Hurts On Monday: Why Pastors Quit & What You Can Do About It*, Churchsmart Resources, 173pp.

Meara, Mary Jane Frances Cavolina et al., (1984) *Growing Up Catholic: An Infinitely Funny Guide for the Faithful, the Fallen, and Everyone In-Between*, A Dolphin Book, 144pp.

Miles, Austin (1990) *Setting the Captives Free: Victims of the Church Tell Their Stories*, Prometheus Books, 239pp.

Milne, Bruce (2007) *Dynamic Diversity: Bridging Class, Age, Race & Gender in the Church*, IVP, 192pp.

Moberg, David O. (1984) *The Church As A Social Institution: The Sociology of American Religion*, 2nd ed., Baker, 602pp.

Moltmann, Jurgen & Kung, Hans eds., (1981) "Who Has the Say in the Church?" *Concilium: Religion in the Eighties*, Seabury Press, 89pp.

Moore, R. Lawrence (1995) *Selling God: American Religion in the Marketplace of Culture*, Oxford University Press, 317pp.

Mueller, John T. (ca. 1970) *My Church & Others: A Summary of the Teachings of the Evangelical Lutheran Church As Distinguished from Those of the Other Denominations*, 6th ed., St. Louis: Adolph Volkening, 92pp.

Niebuhr, H. Richard (1968) *The Social Sources of Denominationalism*, Meridian Books, 12th printing, 304pp.

Noll, Mark; Bebbington, D.W. & Rawlyk, G.A. eds., (1994) *Evangelicalism: Comparative Studies of Popular Protestantism in North America, the British Isles, and Beyond, 1700-1990*, Oxford University Press, 430pp.

Ogden, Greg (2003) *Unfinished Business: Returning the Ministry to the People of God*, Zondervan, 282pp.

Pagels, Elaine (1989) "One God, One Bishop: The Politics of Monotheism," *The Gnostic Gospels*, Vintage Books, pp.28-47.

Parsons, Stephen (2001) *Ungodly Fear: Fundamentalist Christianity & the Abuse of Power*, Lion Pub., 320pp.

Perry, Charles Jr., (1982) *Why Christians Burn Out*, Thomas Nelson, 167pp.

Poling, James N. (1991) *The Abuse of Power: A Theological Problem*, Abingdon, 224pp.

Randall, Robert L. (1988) *Pastor & Parish: The Psychological Core of Ecclesiastical Conflicts*, Human Sciences Press, 172pp.

Reeves, Thomas C. (1998) *The Empty Church: Does Organ-*

ized Religion Matter Anymore?, Touchstone Book, 276pp.

Reid, Clyde (1967) *The Empty Pulpit: A Study in Preaching as Communication*, Harper & Row, 122pp.

Reid, Clyde (1966) *The God-Evaders: How Churches & Their Members Frustrate Genuine Religious Experience*, Harper & Row, 118pp.

Rogers, Adrian (1989) *Depression in the Ministry*, video, Rapha Luncheon, June, Las Vegas, NV.

Rowthorn, Anne (1990) *The Liberation of the Laity*, Morehouse Publishing, 141pp.

Sanders, Brian (2007) *Life After Church: God's Call to Disillusioned Christians*, IVP, 190pp.

Sanford, John A. (1982) *Ministry Burnout*, Paulist Press, 117pp.

Schanz, John P. (1977) *A Theology of Community*, University Press of America, 309pp.

Scheller, Christine A. (2007) "Sorrow But No Regrets: My Life in the Troubled, Redemptive Church," *Christianity Today*, July, pp.40-41.

Schuller, David S. et al., eds, (1980) *Ministry in America: A Report & Analysis, based on an in-depth survey of 47 denominations in the U.S. & Canada, with interpretation by 18 experts*, Harper & Row, 582pp.

Schultze, Quentin J. (1991) *Televangelism & American Culture: The Business of Popular Religion*, Baker, 264pp.

Scott, Ernest F. (1941) *The Nature of the Early Church*, Scribner's, 245pp.

St. Clair, Robert James (1963) *Neurotics in the Church*, Revell, 251pp.

Stafford, Tim (2003) "Hearing Voices: How Can You Tell a Prophet from a Fruitcake?," *Books & Culture*, Sept.-Oct., pp.10-11.

Ulstein, Stefan (1993) *Pastors (Off the Record): Straight Talk About Life in the Ministry*, IVP, 246pp.

Viola, Frank & Barna, George (2008) *Pagan Christianity: Exploring the Roots of Our Church Practices*, Tyndale, 291pp.

Wachtel, Paul L. (1989) "Wealth as a Substitute for Faith & Community," *The Poverty of Affluence: A Psychological Portrait of the American Way of Life*, New Society Publishers, pp.65-79.

Weber, Martin (1995) *Who's Got the truth? Making Sense Out of 5 Different Adventist Gospels*, Calvary Connections, 271pp.

Wecks, John (1996) *Free to Disagree: Moving Beyond the Arguments Over Christian Liberty*, Kregel, 144pp.

Westfall, William (2003) "How Should a Church Look," *Books & Culture*, Sept.-Oct., p.33. A review of *When Church Became Theatre: The Transformation of Evangelical Architcture & Worship in 19th Century America* by Jeanne Halgren Kilde.

Williams, Don (1993) *Jesus & Addiction: A Prescription to Transform the Dysfunctional Church & Recover Authentic Christianity*, Recovery Publications, 197pp.

Wooding, Dan (2004) "Ministry Burnout: Coming to a Pastor Near You!," *Christian News*, Nov.22, p.9.

Zdero, Rad (2006) *The Global House Church Movement*, Navigator Ministries, 141pp.

Zens, Jon (2001) "Authoritarianism in the Church: The Abuse of Leadership," *Searching Together*, 29:2-3, 37pp.

Zens, Jon (1995) "The 'Clergy/Laity' Distinction: Help or Hindrance to the Body of Christ?" *Searching Together*, 23:4, 15pp.

Zens, Jon (1981) *The Pastor*, BREM, 9pp.

Appendix

These questions were sent to Jon Zens regarding this book from Eldra Bunkley in North Carolina who reviewed an early copy of the work.

Hi Jon,

Here are some thoughts and questions regarding your book. I really like how you divided the specific subjects. This makes the info easier to read and organize in my mind. It was good to address the issues that probably an average American church go-er experiences. I could easily personalize the issues.

1. Do you have a specific target group you are writing to?

JZ's Answer: I am reaching out to all kinds of folks—but at least to people who wonder what church is all about, to people who may have been hurt by churches, to people who have never darkened the door of a church building, and to believers who are seeking to sharpen their vision of Christ's kingdom.

2. Sometimes your generalizations made me ask, "what proof does Jon have for this statement?" such as on page 27, "More often than not, pride, self-will and malicious gossip will be found in the roots of these divisions." and on page 44, "Because so many churches are built around the pastor's charisma. . ."

JZ's Answer: In these two instances, I think the statements are incontestable. Who would deny that somebody's arrogance and self-will are foundational to most church splits? The dependence of most churches on "the pastor's" aura is demonstrable from any number of angles. To illustrate the pervasiveness of pastor-dependence, consider the utter chaos that would ensue if the pastors of the most-attended 500 churches in America tendered their immediate resignations. The instant plunge in giving and attendance would be staggering. Many very sharp people have read this manuscript and no one has questioned the two points you isolate.

3. Should you give more ink to address those pastors who are trying to make the best of a bad system to encourage them?

> **JZ's Answer:** I could, but that is not the purpose of this book. Truthfully, it would be very difficult for me in good conscience to encourage them to make the best of a bad system. That system is literally ruining and killing husbands, wives and families every day. There are many lovely, humble servants within the clergy-system. I know a number of them personally. My hope is that the Lord Jesus is leading his sheep into a deeper relationship with him.

4. It seems the only solution to the traditional church is for people to leave it. But aren't there some things we can do to minister to our brothers and sisters who won't leave for whatever reason? It seems there has to be some wider solutions to give to those who will remain there.

> **JZ's Answer:** The Lord's ways will come to different levels of expression in each church structure. Some structures are very stifling and others have more freedom. The tragedy, however, is that most churches do not cultivate a soil in which Christ's truth can take root. The truth can only go so far and then it will meet resistance, often with a vengeance. Sadly, then, "solutions" do not fare very well in institutional churches. People with insight end up functioning the best they can, knowing there are boundaries that cannot be crossed without serious

consequences. Many folks are quite happy with the existing structures, and that is fine. We must love all the brethren, and serve them in any way we can. I accept people because of our oneness in Christ, not based on their view of how churches should function. Broadly speaking, it is by loving people and doing good that evil is overthrown and falsehood exposed.

5. What do you mean by just because God has used the pastor-centered system doesn't mean He sanctions it?

JZ's Answer: We know that the Lord uses the governments of the world to accomplish his purposes, but that does not mean he sanctions all of their actions. For God to "sanction" something means that he is behind it, approves of it, and has revealed for it to be done. This cannot be said about the pastor-centered system. There is no evidence in the NT to suggest that the Lord sanctions a pastor-centered system. But he still uses it to accomplish many purposes. Here is an example that may help a little. The musical, "Jesus Christ, Superstar," contains some truth and outright falsehood about Jesus. My guess is that the Lord used that production in some people's lives as a step in their full discovery of salvation in Christ. Did God "sanction" this musical? I don't think so. The truth is, the Lord uses a number of things that he does not sanction. Our goal should be to function in step with what we know he has sanctioned!

6. Doesn't every group think it is closer to the truth than other groups, including our own?

JZ's Answer: Your question raises a very important point. The problem is this: church history reveals that when alleged insight comes to a group it usually brings them to separate from other believers in an exclusive manner. Each of us has to follow the truth the Lord shows us. But the acid test is, "does the way I hold my convictions increase my love for all of Christ's people or make me reclusive?" We are deceived if we think that in getting "closer to the truth" we must sever our relationships with other believers. Jesus is in the business of giving light to his people. It is our responsibility to pursue such light in humility, knowing that anything we "know," we do not know it as we should.

7. Here is the most important question I have for you over all the rest—Shouldn't every and any teacher of God's Word make a disclaimer that states, "there are flaws in my theology"? Even though we strongly believe certain things to be true, can't any of us be wrong?

> **JZ's Answer:** Absolutely. All of us are in the process of growing. We will always be disciples at Jesus' feet, listening to his counsel. As Thomas Dubay points out in his superb book, *Caring: A Biblical Theology of Community*, we must all be willing to bend in the light of solid evidence, embrace our views with humility, and always be open to correction. "No one," Dubay observes, "adequately represents the Lord. Despite my grandest aspirations and my best efforts, I am perilously close to zero; without the Lord I am zero. He is infinite; I am finite to the tip of my toes. . . . No one of us has a corner on light or goodness" (*Searching Together*, 14:4, 1985, p.6). The other side of the coin, however, is that just because the possibility exists for any of us to be wrong does not rule out the possibility that any of us can also actually communicate the truth in love.

Endnotes

A Church Building Every 1/2 Mile:

1. *The Irresistible Revolution*, Zondervan, 2006, p.37.
2. *Judged By the Gospel: A Review of Adventism*, Verdict Publications, 1980, pp.325, 359.
3. "Religion & Materialism: 1950-1970," *Religion in America Since 1945: A History*, Columbia University Press, 2005, pp.40-41.
4. *The Shelter of Each Other*, Grosset/Putnam, 1996, p.39.
5. *Smoke on the Mountain*, written by Connie Ray, produced by special arrangement with Samuel French, Inc., 1990.
6. *The True Nature of a Gospel Church*, edited and abridged by John Huxtable, London, 1947, p.55.
7. William Barclay, *The Letters to the Corinthians*, revised edition, Westminster Press, 1977, p.134.
8. *Working the Angles: The Shape of Pastoral Integrity*, Eerdmans, 1987, p.4; cited in N. Shawchuck & R. Heuser, *Leading the Congregation*, Abingdon, 1993, p.40.
9. *Heroes & Heretics: A Social History of Dissent*, Alfred A. Knopf, 1964, p.7.
10. *Pastoral Psychology*, 47:1, Sept., 1998, pp.49-67; cf. H. Michael Rich, "The Interrelationships of Leisure Attitude, Leisure Satisfaction, Leisure Behavior, Intrinsic Motivation and Burnout Among Clergy," 1995 Ph.D. Dissertation, University of Maryland, College Park, MD.
11. One pastor's conference scheduled for 2008 said in their brochure, "We intentionally seek to foster a male fraternity because it is rare and uniquely refreshing for pastors to fellowship with men who carry similar burdens and to counsel

one another with the kind of frankness that is awkward to do in mixed company. However, we do not prohibit wives from attending, knowing that there are circumstances where it is the best choice for marriage or ministry."

12. "The Ministry's Gordian Knot," *Leadership*, 1:1, Winter, 1980, pp.50-51.
13. Nov., 1995, p.4.
14. "Depression in the Ministry," Rapha Video, Las Vegas, NV, 1989.
15. Phil Fischer, "Save Me," *New Believer*, Apple Hill Records, 2007; www.philfischer.com.
16. "Churchianity Today," www.watchman.net.
17. *Your Church Can Grow*, Regal, 1979, pp.66, 67.
18. Janet Fishburn, "Male Clergy Adultery as Vocational Confusion," *Christian Century*, September 15-22, 1982, p.922; www.religion-online.org.
19. "Defeating the Demons: The Prevention of Clergy Sexual Abuse," *Christian Ethics Today*, 6:5, October, 2000; www.christianethicstoday.com.
20. Matthew Klein, "Meet the Pastor – Pastor Demographics," *American Demographics*, April, 1998.
21. Peter Steinfels, "More Dismissals for Southern Baptist Pastors," *The New York Times*, Dec.4, 1998. Emphasis mine.
22. *The Liberation of the Laity*, Morehouse Publishing, 1990, p.24.
23. 10/19/07; www.themordecaiproject.com).
24. William Warren Sweet, "The Rise of Theological Schools in America," *Church History*, 6:3, 1937, p.260.
25. Mike Parker, "The Basic Meaning of 'Elder' in the New Testament," *Baptist Reformation Review*, 7:2, 1978, pp.33-46.
26. *The Liberation of the Laity*, p.15.

27. *The Letters to the Corinthians*, revised edition, p.134.

28. Jon Zens, "Each According to His Ability: Principles of New Covenant Giving," *Baptist Reformation Review*, 8:2, 1979; "Perspectives on New Covenant Giving," *Searching Together*, 16:4, 1987; Tom Atkinson, "There's Gold in Them Thar Pews: A Review of *Pastor Driven Stewardship*," *Searching Together*, 34:2-4, 2006.

29. Cited in Rodney Stark, *The Rise of Christianity*, Harper/Collins, 1997, p.207.

30. *The Comfortable Pew*, J.B. Lippincott, 1965, p.xviii).

31. *From State Church to Pluralism*, Macmillan, 1962, p.11. See also, Stephen Neill, *Colonialism & Christian Missions*, McGraw-Hill, 1966; James A. Scherer, *Missionary, Go Home!*, Prentice-Hall, 1964; Jon Zens, "The Bible in One Hand, and A Flag in the Other: Joining Gospel & Country Sours the Great Commission," *Searching Together*, 20:4, 1992, pp.12-17.

32. Source: Dr. Ralph Neighbour, from an unpublished manuscript.

33. *Listening to Your Life: Daily Meditations with Frederick Buechner*, HarperOne, 1992, pp.331-332.

34. http://www.ptmin.org/bethany.pdf

35. *The Comfortable Pew*, p.76.

36. *The Comfortable Pew*, p.xxv.

37. Tyndale, 2005, 144pp.

38. *Newsletter,* Plain Truth Ministries, September, 2007.

39. H. Richard Niebuhr, *The Social Sources of Denominationalism*, Meridian Books, 1969, p.3.

Four Tragic Shifts:

1. *History of Christian Ethics*, Vol. 1, Augsburg Pub. House, 1979, pp. 39-40.
2. *Traditions, Tensions, Transitions in Ministry*, Twenty-Third Publications, 1982, p. 54.
3. *Traditions, Tensions, Transitions in Ministry*, p.30.
4. Cincinnati: Jenning & Graham, 1906, 382pp.
5. New York: Anchor Doubleday, 1967, 577pp.
6. *The History of Christian Doctrines*, Banner of Truth, 1978, p.87.
7. "The Westminster Confession of Faith," *The Standard Bearer*, Oct. 1, 1979, p.17.
8. *Eucharist and Church Fellowship in the First Four Centuries*, Concordia Pub. House, 1966, pp. 66-67.
9. *The Letters to the Corinthians*, Revised Edition, Westminster Press, 1975, pp. 133-134.
10. *The True Believer*, Mentor Books, 1964, pp.100-101.
11. *Unity and Diversity in the New Testament*, Westminster Press, 1977, p.351.

More Endorsements

I have received hundreds of emails from all over the world. People who find themselves disconnected from what is currently perceived as "church." The questions are all the same: "Why do I feel like there is more?"—"Why am I not spiritually growing and fulfilled?"—"Why, in a religion that stresses intimate relationships, can I not find a single long-lasting friend?" If you, like thousands of others, are asking such questions, I would highly recommend this book.

> – **Andy Zoppelt**, former pastor, currently teaches and has a web presence at www.TheRealChurch.com, Florida

Wow, I just finished reading it, and I love it! It needs to be passed on! This little book is long overdue in a world where the respect and beauty of the Body of Christ has faded. Finally someone points out the root of sin behind it all. Clear and vibrant, this overview gives careful diagnosis, vivid examples, and allows the truth of the Bible to speak. This book is a great starting point for discussion—a small treasure to jump-start our thinking and praying toward glorious change.

> – **Raymond Faber**, M.D., Pennsylvania

This book comes as a timely intervention by Jon Zens in the midst of the current controversy surrounding Frank Viola's *Pagan Christianity*. Jon calls us to stop depending on "the pastor" and to start *being* the ekklesia of Christ. Deconstructing his way through church buildings and other debris from our evangelical past he clearly shows the need to re-form the "community of the King" and to once more demonstrate the reality or "truth" of the life of Christ formed in a called people.

> – **Doug Hefferman**, Celtic Prayer Centre, Cork, Ireland

It is fitting that Jon should write along these lines in his *A Church Bldg Every 1/2 Mile*, for he is in touch with the problems that plague the Christian community and is constantly in search of the right answers. It is proper that a freethinker like him should give attention to this subject, for he is in the position to speak the language of the common man. It is likewise in order that a gallant man should write upon this subject, for he has tasted the bitterness of sectarianism and misunderstanding.

– **Buff Scott, Jr.**, Author of *Mad Church Disease* & the E-Newsletter, *Reformation Rumblings*, Arizona

Jon is a uniquely observant commentator on American Christianity. He has spent decades both observing and analyzing the oddities of the post-reformation church from an unrelentingly biblical point of view. This collection of essays contains some of the most penetrating of his work. When Jon turns his x-ray machine on the contemporary Christian church, we find out just how far its bones are out of alignment with its source.

– **Hal Miller**, author of *Christian Community: Biblical or Optional?*

Jon Zens has focused his Polaroid and given us a telling snapshot of life on Christian Main Street. "What makes American Christianity tick?" The same thing that makes Wal-Mart, the Mall of America and Starbucks keep ticking—focus on the "customer," the best locations, and above all, plenty of choice. Tragically, the Church has chosen to compete with the marketplace, so is it any wonder the world passes her by, and is only occasionally impressed by what is offered? Everybody knows the *true* marketplace does a much better job!

– **Charles Wilhelm**, Germany, author of *Biblical Dyslexia: Overcoming the Barriers to Understanding Scripture*

For those interested in functioning outside of the institutional church, www.HouseChurchResource.org provides a wealth of articles and information to help foster research, reflection and action.

If you would like to contact Jon with questions or dialog about this book, write: jzens@searchingtogether.org or call him at either 715-338-2796 or 651-465-6516.

Printed in the United States
121264LV00001B/1-132/P